CAMPBELL MOR

MW00388448

The Best Paper Aircraft

—New and Expanded!

A Perigee Book

Contents

Introduction

Welcome to The Best Paper Aircraft—Revised and Expanded *—just when you thought it was safe at last to enter the classroom! Because of the first volume of* The Best Paper Aircraft, *thousands of happy students, business people, politicians, funeral directors, doctors and others are now enjoying their newfound hobby of building paper aircraft. However, if you missed out on all the fun, or you just want to strive for higher technical skill and versatility, this book is for you!*

Although these models are challenging, almost anyone can make a superior paper plane by observing the easy-to-follow instructions.
Learn how to construct a fantastic Stunt Fly, revolutionary Heliglider and even a Space Shuttle, for those space-hungry venturers.
Almost all the flying devices shown in this book are folded; you don't have to spend endless hours sticking bits of cardboard on as ballast, or cutting here, there and everywhere. All you need is one sheet of paper: 8½ × 11 or 8½ × 14 is ideal. So now students can rip into their note books to create instant gliders in any situation.

Paper folding, or origami as it is better known, originated in Japan hundreds of years ago. It had many ceremonial and decorative purposes. Today, it is used to imitate almost anything on this planet and beyond. With paper aircraft, you have the satisfaction of using your creation, rather than just sitting it on the shelf.
So grab a sheet of paper and put your concentration to the test — you'll be more than pleased with the results.

Clubs and Competitions

Clubs are ideal for school students who wish to pool their resources and design new aircraft. These designs can lead to new and even better inventions with paper — all you need is a little imagination! Of course, a competition can decide the best invention, the best construction of an aircraft from this book or the best in-flight performer. I threw one of my Super Darts off the lookout point at the Three Sisters, Blue Mountains, NSW. It took 29 minutes to reach the bottom. A competition for the longest airborne dart or, say, the fastest dart or even the best stunt performer can be held at your school or university.

Types of Paper to Use

All the aircraft in this book use 8½ × 11 or 8½ × 14 paper.

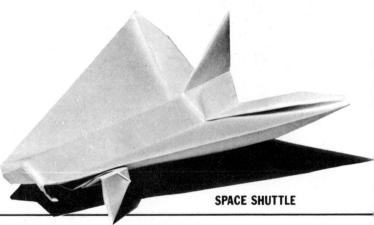

SPACE SHUTTLE

EXPLANATION OF SYMBOLS

The symbols are very important if you are to succeed when folding. The following symbols will be used throughout this book. Before you start folding your first winner, a little practice with small pieces of paper will help.

Larger view of previous diagram.

Smaller view of previous diagram.

When this valley fold has a dotted line it means that the rest of the fold is hidden under a flap etcetera.

Push in.

Fold in general direction of arrow.

Turn the model over.

Sectional view — only that part of the diagram necessary for the fold is shown.

Crease-fold — fold in direction of arrow, then unfold.

Detailed view to be shown.

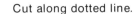

Stair-step fold.

Cut along dotted line.

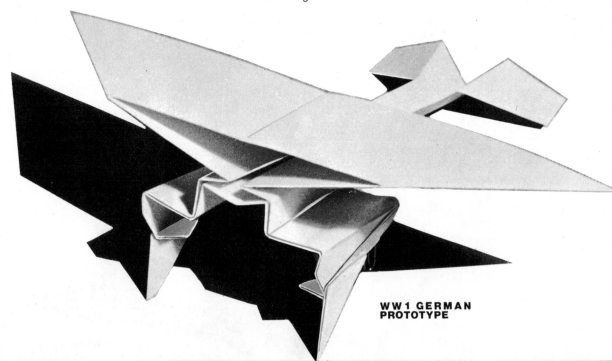

WW 1 GERMAN PROTOTYPE

FOLDING TECHNIQUES

Getting the fold right is only half the job. The real skill is in throwing the completed dart. As you will discover, each aircraft requires a special throwing technique.

Finally, take it slowly, fold accurately and throw with precision — it's bound to provoke a reaction from fellow students and friends!

1

Valley fold (indicated by a line of dashes) — fold in direction of arrow along the line of dashes.

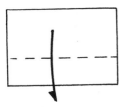

2

Mountain fold (indicated by a line of dots and dashes) — fold in direction of arrow BEHIND YOU along the line of dots and dashes.

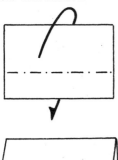

3

Reverse fold — crease along the dotted line and fold outwards as shown.

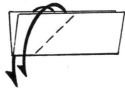

4

Inverse fold — crease along the dotted line and push inwards as shown.

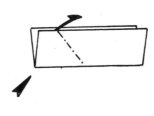
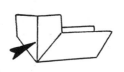
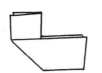

5

"Rabbit ear" fold — make creases and then fold the two sides inwards, bringing them to touch the bottom line and forming a point or "ear".

(top and side view)

PAPER PLANE BASE FOLDS

Later in this book you will come across more complicated aircraft that start with one of these base folds. It is essential that you learn them first before embarking on the more complicated models. These base folds are also the foundation for making new and even more complicated designs of your own. A little practice and imagination can go a long way!

Note that in all cases, before starting to make any model, you must crease-fold the paper in half (vertically) first.

BASE FOLD NO. 1

This is the simplest of the base folds. When doing the mountain fold, it is easiest to turn the paper over (the mountain fold becomes a valley fold), then turn the paper back over and push your finger into the point where all the creases meet. The sides should pop up making it easy to complete the base fold.

1.
Fold and crease the valley folds AD and BC, then the mountain fold EF.

2.
Move the sides inwards, bringing the top edge downwards.

3.
The completed fold.

BASE FOLD No. 2

1.
Have the top corners folded down as in a normal dart.

2.
With B as the axis, bring point A down to align with side BD as shown and crease. Repeat on the other side with C as the axis. Mountain fold where shown.

3.
Bring in the sides and top.

4.
The completed base fold.

BASE FOLD No. 3

1.
Fold down the top corners first as for Base Fold No. 2. Then unfold them and fold the top edges down to meet the creases thus left.

2.
With B as the axis bring point A down to align with side BD as shown and crease. Repeat on the other side with C as the axis. Mountain fold where shown.

3.
Bring in top and sides.

4.
The completed base fold.

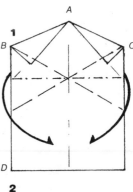

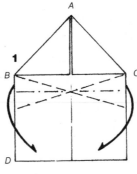

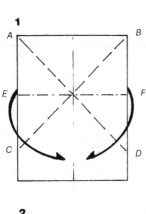

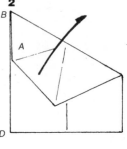

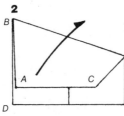

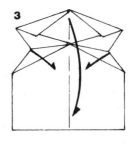

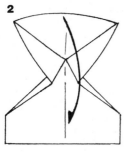

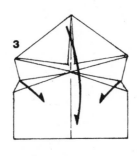

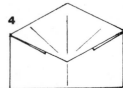

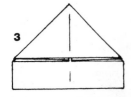

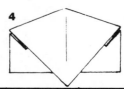

Easier Aircraft

long distance glider

If you're sitting way at the back of a lecture theatre or cinema, this dart will help you to "get your message across"!

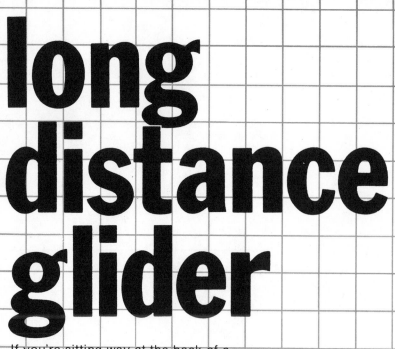

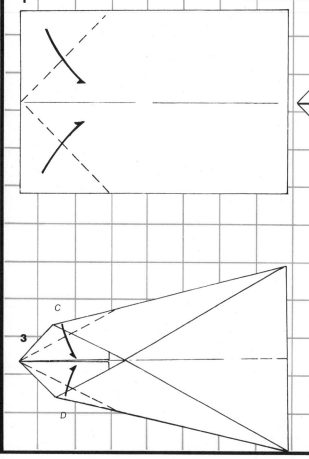

1.

Use a sheet of 8½ × 11 or 8½ × 14 paper. Remember, when making any dart, crease-fold the paper in half first. Fold the top corners down.

2.

Fold in the sides, making sure points A and B meet each other at the centre crease.

3.

Fold in points C and D. The top two edges should meet each other at the centre crease.

4.

Mountain fold the model in half.

5.

Fold the wings down to meet the bottom edge of the fuselage.

6.

The completed dart. Curl the tail section up slightly for lift if necessary. If model is too light, inverse fold the nose by about 1 inch.

THROWING SUGGESTIONS

Throw with gentle force at approximately 30 to 40 degrees in an upward direction. Because of its length, this dart should prove accurate in meeting its target.

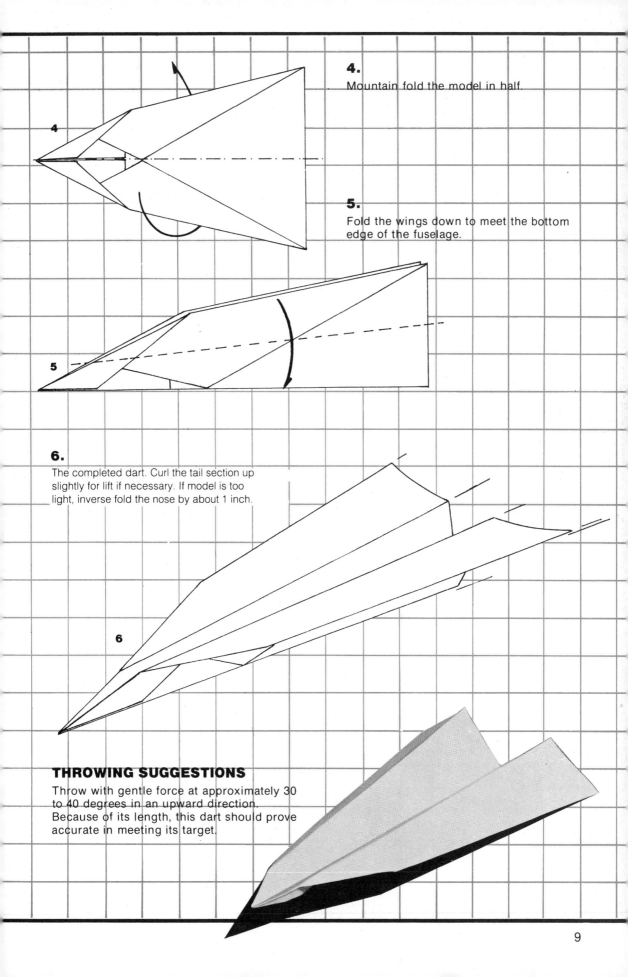

super wing

An incredible paper wing! It is surprisingly stable and can perform some stunts too. Works best as a glider.

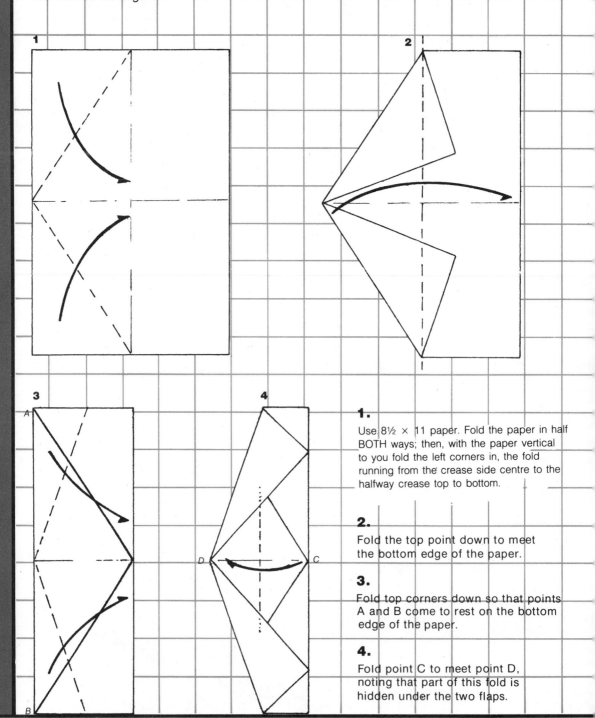

1.

Use 8½ × 11 paper. Fold the paper in half BOTH ways; then, with the paper vertical to you fold the left corners in, the fold running from the crease side centre to the halfway crease top to bottom.

2.

Fold the top point down to meet the bottom edge of the paper.

3.

Fold top corners down so that points A and B come to rest on the bottom edge of the paper.

4.

Fold point C to meet point D, noting that part of this fold is hidden under the two flaps.

10

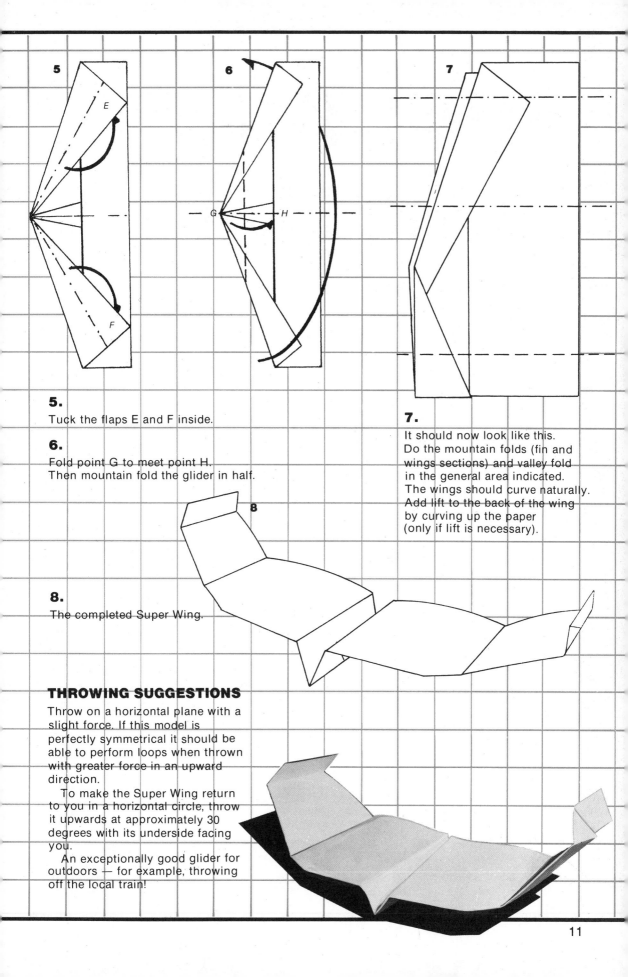

5.
Tuck the flaps E and F inside.

6.
Fold point G to meet point H.
Then mountain fold the glider in half.

7.
It should now look like this.
Do the mountain folds (fin and
wings sections) and valley fold
in the general area indicated.
The wings should curve naturally.
Add lift to the back of the wing
by curving up the paper
(only if lift is necessary).

8.
The completed Super Wing.

THROWING SUGGESTIONS

Throw on a horizontal plane with a
slight force. If this model is
perfectly symmetrical it should be
able to perform loops when thrown
with greater force in an upward
direction.

To make the Super Wing return
to you in a horizontal circle, throw
it upwards at approximately 30
degrees with its underside facing
you.

An exceptionally good glider for
outdoors — for example, throwing
off the local train!

split nose cone dart

Here is a dart that can be thrown with greater force because of its solidly constructed nose section. I threw one off the top of a hotel at Surfers Paradise. It was airborne for a long time and travelled a fair distance.

1

2

A   **B**

3

4

1.

Use a sheet of 8½ × 11 or 8½ × 14 paper. Fold the top corners down

2.

Mountain fold where indicated. This is best done by turning the paper over and valley folding, swinging the flaps A and B around.

3.

Crease where indicated and make "rabbit ears" (as shown in Folding Techniques on page 4) on each side.

4.

Fold the top point behind, raising forward the two "rabbit ears". These are to become the split nose cone of this model.

5.
Mountain fold the dart in half.

6.
Fold wings down so that their edges meet the bottom edge of the fuselage.

7.
The completed dart. Curl up the tail section for lift if necessary.

THROWING SUGGESTIONS
Throw upwards with some force, preferably against the wind.

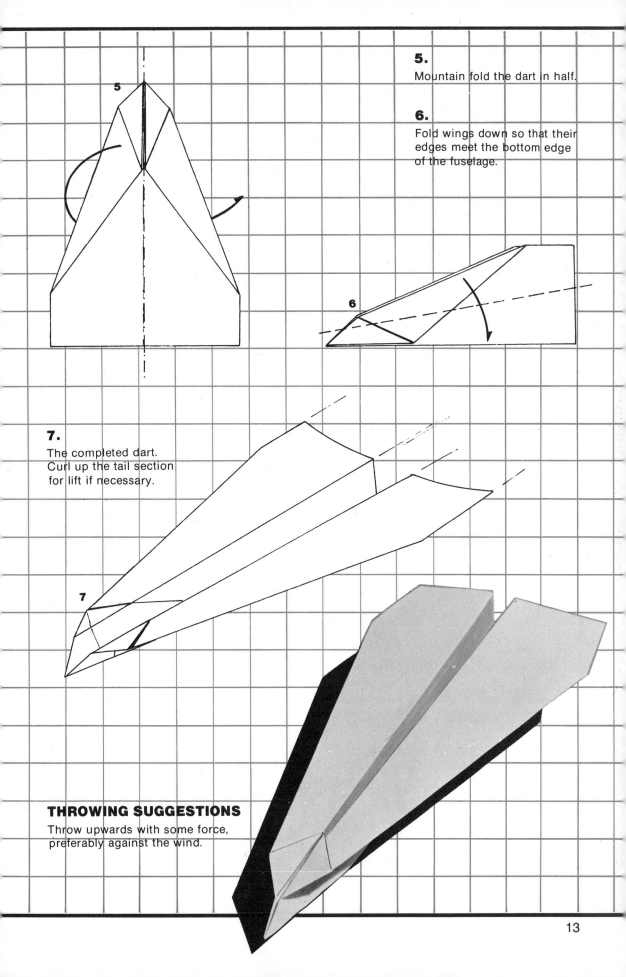

super dart

Folded correctly, this dart can perform huge loops 9 to 10 yards in diameter or travel great distances. Its heavy nose cone can be slightly raised to give the greater forward lift necessary for loop performance.

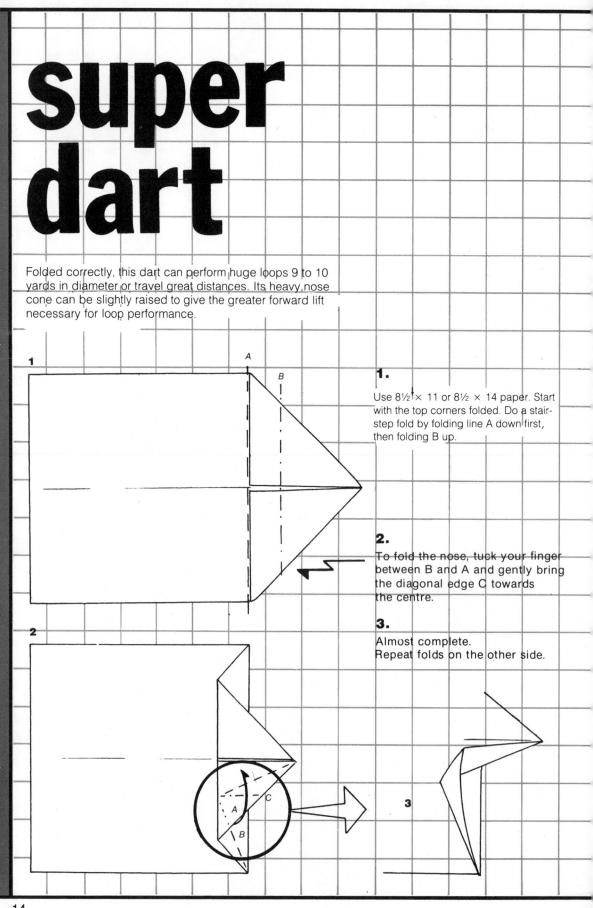

1.

Use 8½ × 11 or 8½ × 14 paper. Start with the top corners folded. Do a stair-step fold by folding line A down first, then folding B up.

2.

To fold the nose, tuck your finger between B and A and gently bring the diagonal edge C towards the centre.

3.

Almost complete.
Repeat folds on the other side.

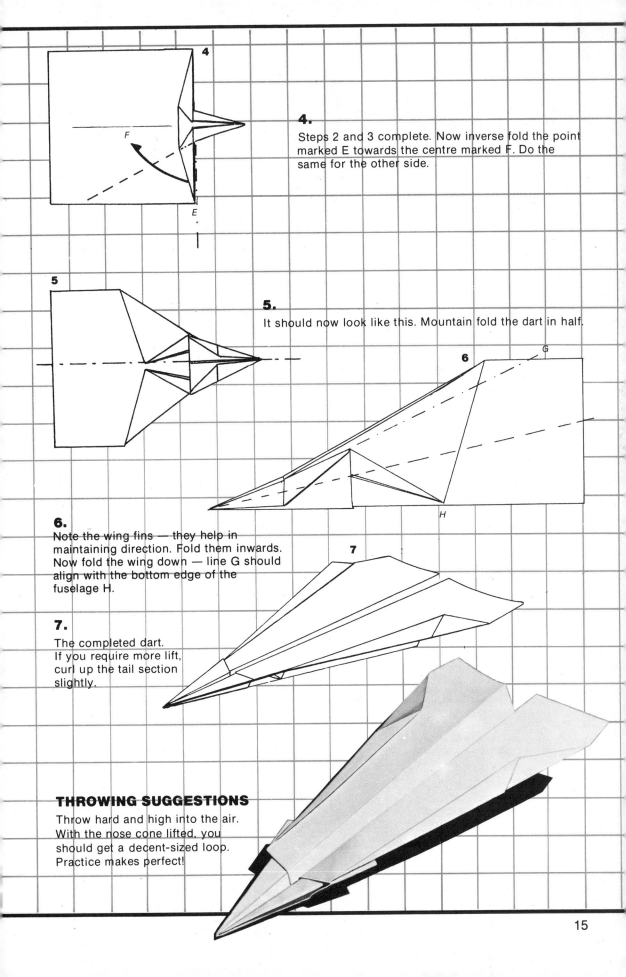

4.

Steps 2 and 3 complete. Now inverse fold the point marked E towards the centre marked F. Do the same for the other side.

5.

It should now look like this. Mountain fold the dart in half.

6.

Note the wing fins — they help in maintaining direction. Fold them inwards. Now fold the wing down — line G should align with the bottom edge of the fuselage H.

7.

The completed dart.
If you require more lift, curl up the tail section slightly.

THROWING SUGGESTIONS

Throw hard and high into the air. With the nose cone lifted, you should get a decent-sized loop. Practice makes perfect!

super looper

Here's a dart that will have heads rotating on their shoulders!

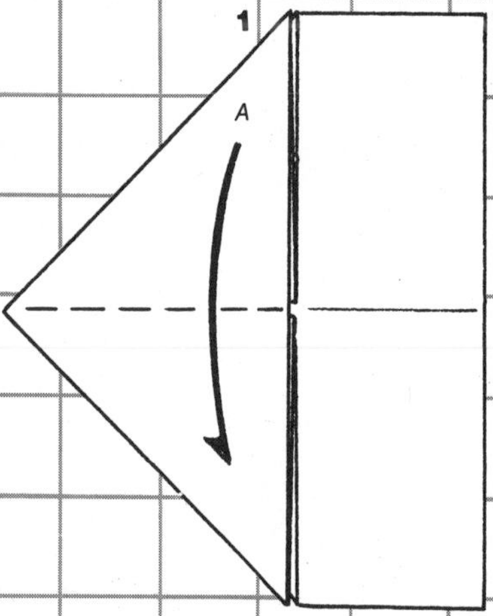

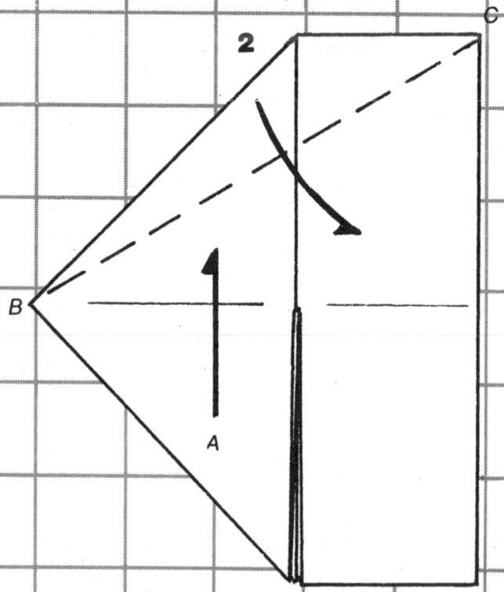

1.

Use 8½ × 11 paper. Begin with Base Fold No. 1 (page 6). Fold the top flap A down.

2.

Fold along line BC, then fold flap A back over. Repeat these steps for the left-hand side.

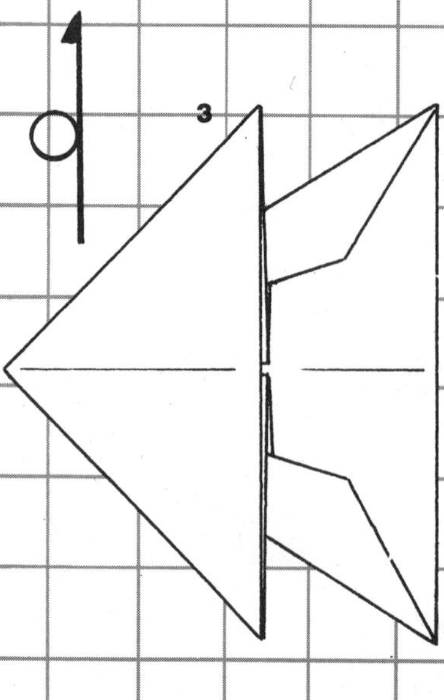

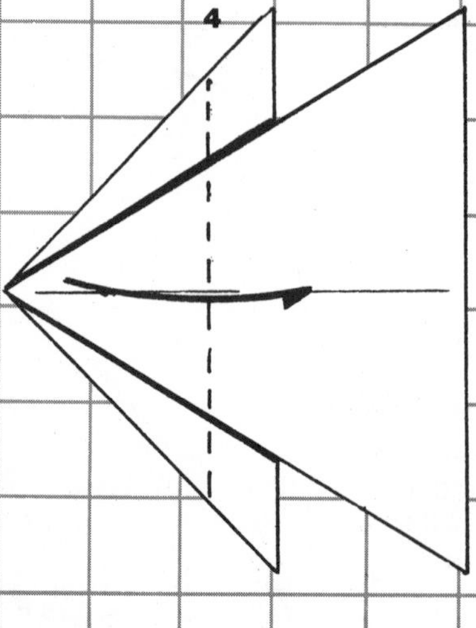

3.

Step 2 completed. Turn the model over.

4.

Fold the top down approximately where indicated.

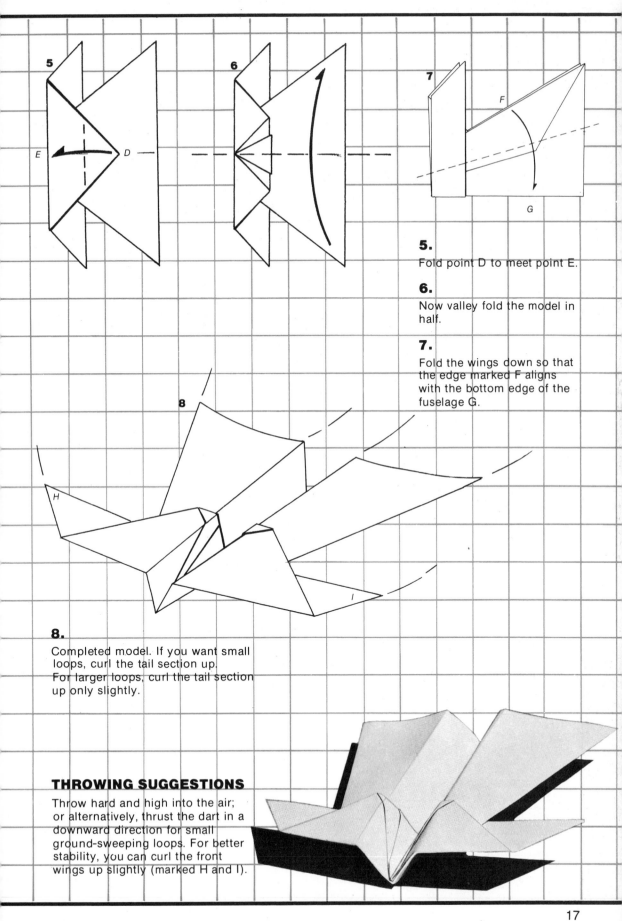

5.
Fold point D to meet point E.

6.
Now valley fold the model in half.

7.
Fold the wings down so that the edge marked F aligns with the bottom edge of the fuselage G.

8.
Completed model. If you want small loops, curl the tail section up. For larger loops, curl the tail section up only slightly.

THROWING SUGGESTIONS

Throw hard and high into the air; or alternatively, thrust the dart in a downward direction for small ground-sweeping loops. For better stability, you can curl the front wings up slightly (marked H and I).

WW1 German prototype

Not only a novelty — but flyable! If the lesson is aviation history, show your appreciation by landing one of these on the teacher's desk.

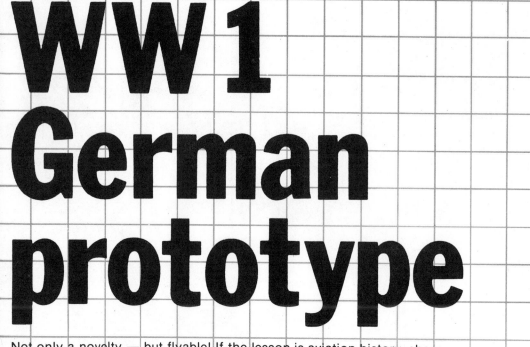

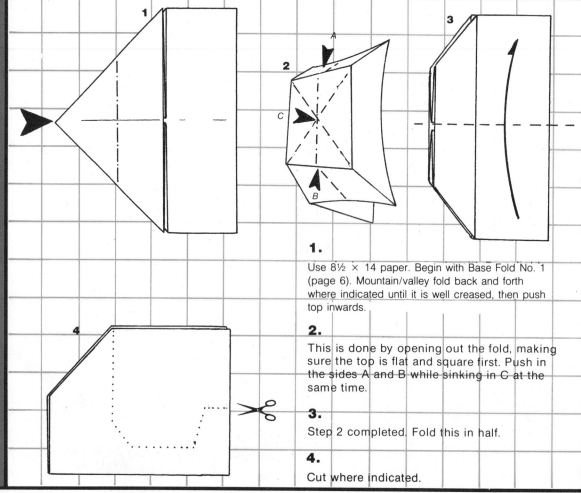

1.

Use 8½ × 14 paper. Begin with Base Fold No. 1 (page 6). Mountain/valley fold back and forth where indicated until it is well creased, then push top inwards.

2.

This is done by opening out the fold, making sure the top is flat and square first. Push in the sides A and B while sinking in C at the same time.

3.

Step 2 completed. Fold this in half.

4.

Cut where indicated.

5.
Fold wing down.

6.
Fold up.

7.
Fold down again.

8.
Close-up view of undercarriage
section assembly.
Fold as indicated.

9.
Fold top flap down again.

10.
Swing the whole undercarriage
section up.

11.
The top point must be folded down.
This will ensure the undercarriage
supports the plane. Repeat steps 5 to 11 on
the other wing.

12.
Bring the wings down, grasping each end at
point D and pull to straighten wingspan.
Undercarriage should be lowered in position.
Fold the tail wings down at an angle.

13.
The completed WW1 plane.

THROWING SUGGESTIONS

With your index finger inside the
fuselage at the end of the plane,
grasp the outside with your thumb
and forefinger. With a slightly
downward aim, gently let
go of the plane. It will glide to a
soft landing.

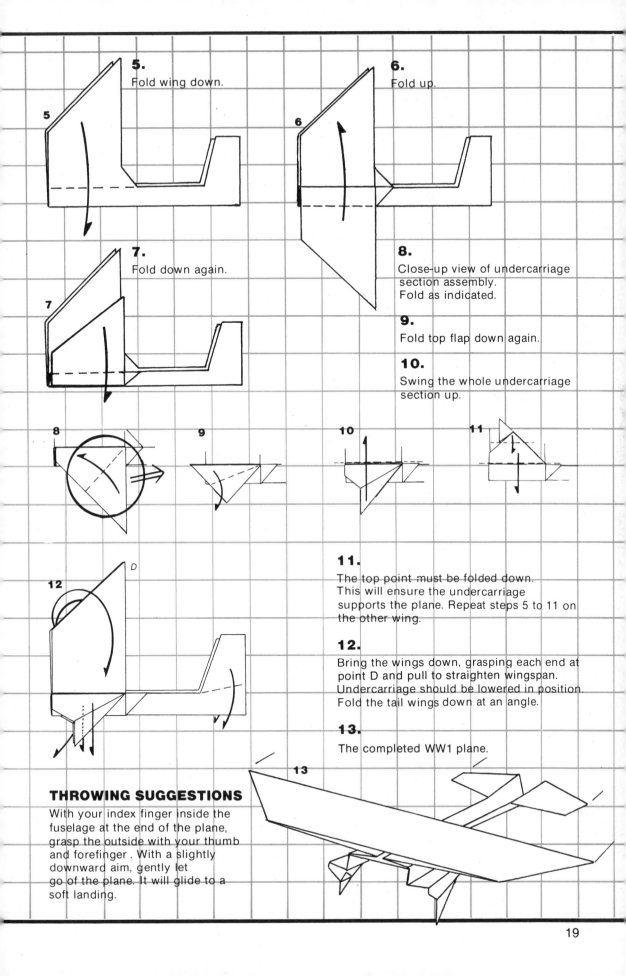

glider
with advanced undercarriage

Here's a delightful yet simple craft that is bound to annoy. What would you do if something with legs (like a giant moth) landed in your hair while you're watching a horror movie? The same undercarriage in this model can be used in the World War 1 plane too.

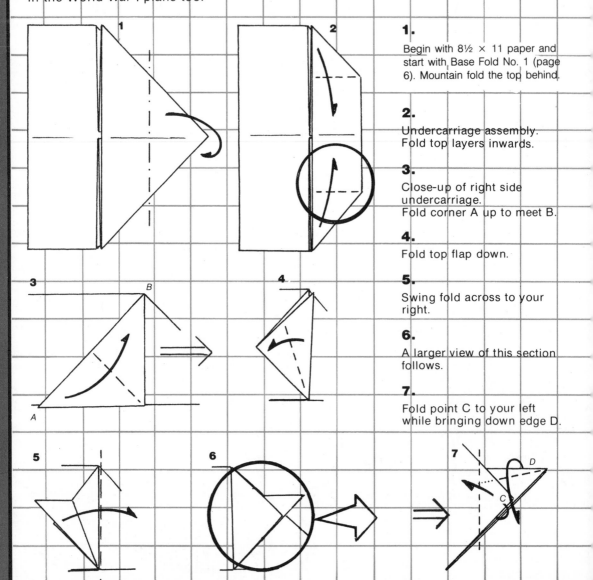

1.

Begin with 8½ × 11 paper and start with Base Fold No. 1 (page 6). Mountain fold the top behind.

2.

Undercarriage assembly. Fold top layers inwards.

3.

Close-up of right side undercarriage. Fold corner A up to meet B.

4.

Fold top flap down.

5.

Swing fold across to your right.

6.

A larger view of this section follows.

7.

Fold point C to your left while bringing down edge D.

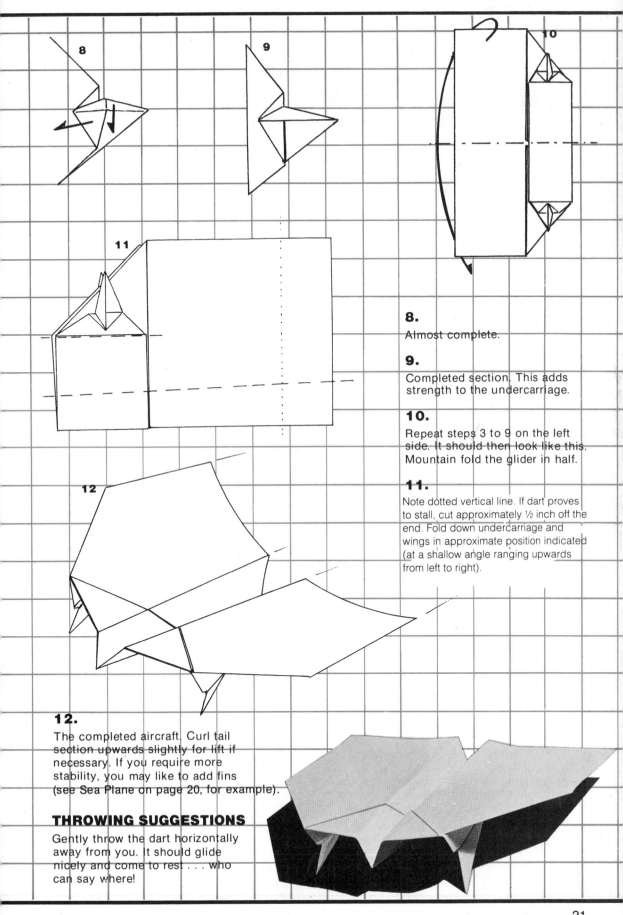

8.

Almost complete.

9.

Completed section. This adds strength to the undercarriage.

10.

Repeat steps 3 to 9 on the left side. It should then look like this. Mountain fold the glider in half.

11.

Note dotted vertical line. If dart proves to stall, cut approximately ½ inch off the end. Fold down undercarriage and wings in approximate position indicated (at a shallow angle ranging upwards from left to right).

12.

The completed aircraft. Curl tail section upwards slightly for lift if necessary. If you require more stability, you may like to add fins (see Sea Plane on page 20, for example).

THROWING SUGGESTIONS

Gently throw the dart horizontally away from you. It should glide nicely and come to rest . . . who can say where!

sea plane

It's called this because of its undercarriage. If you spray it with waterproof lacquer it should be able to land and float in water!

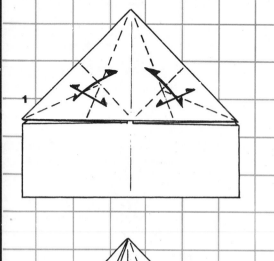

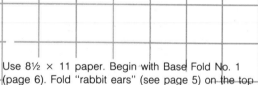

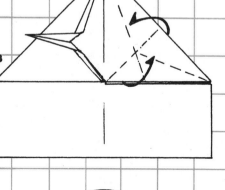

Use 8½ × 11 paper. Begin with Base Fold No. 1 (page 6). Fold "rabbit ears" (see page 5) on the top two flaps.

2.

First crease for "rabbit ears" complete. Open and make second and final crease.

3.

Almost complete. Fold "ear" up and repeat on the right side of the model.

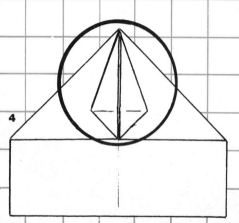

4.

Complete. The section circled is detailed in the following enlarged diagrams of the undercarriage assembly.

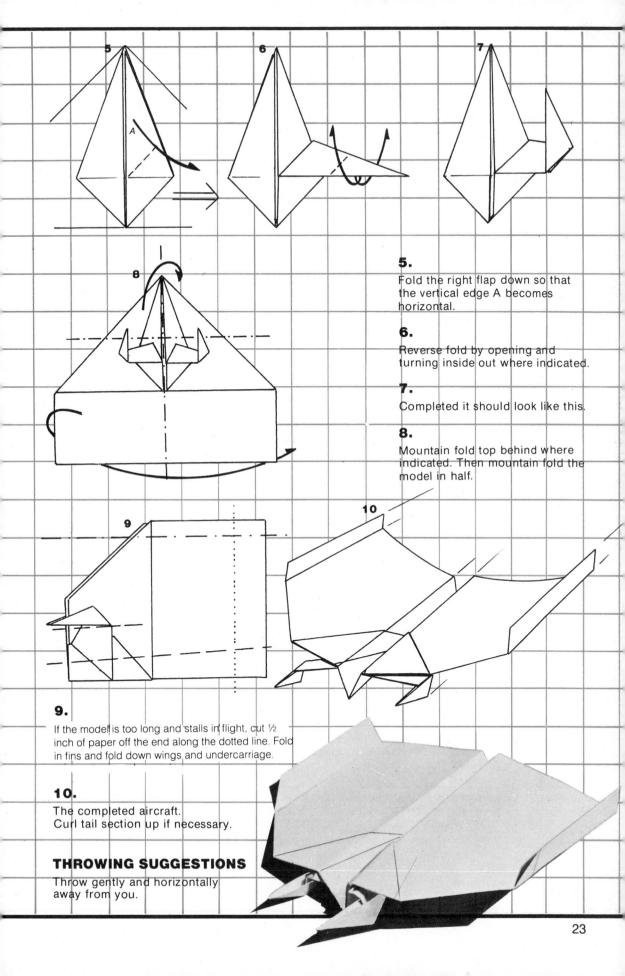

5.

Fold the right flap down so that the vertical edge A becomes horizontal.

6.

Reverse fold by opening and turning inside out where indicated.

7.

Completed it should look like this.

8.

Mountain fold top behind where indicated. Then mountain fold the model in half.

9.

If the model is too long and stalls in flight, cut ½ inch of paper off the end along the dotted line. Fold in fins and fold down wings and undercarriage.

10.

The completed aircraft.
Curl tail section up if necessary.

THROWING SUGGESTIONS

Throw gently and horizontally away from you.

shuttle copter

Here's one that can be thrown high into the air with speed, and yet it spins gently down to earth. Great for those outdoor concerts or school assemblies! Where it lands . . . who knows?

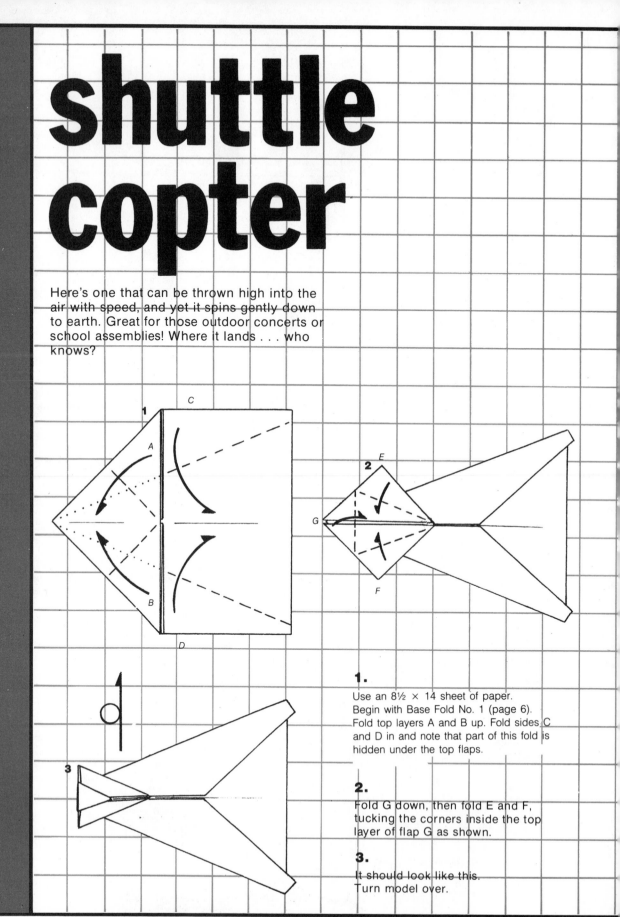

1.

Use an 8½ × 14 sheet of paper. Begin with Base Fold No. 1 (page 6). Fold top layers A and B up. Fold sides C and D in and note that part of this fold is hidden under the top flaps.

2.

Fold G down, then fold E and F, tucking the corners inside the top layer of flap G as shown.

3.

It should look like this. Turn model over.

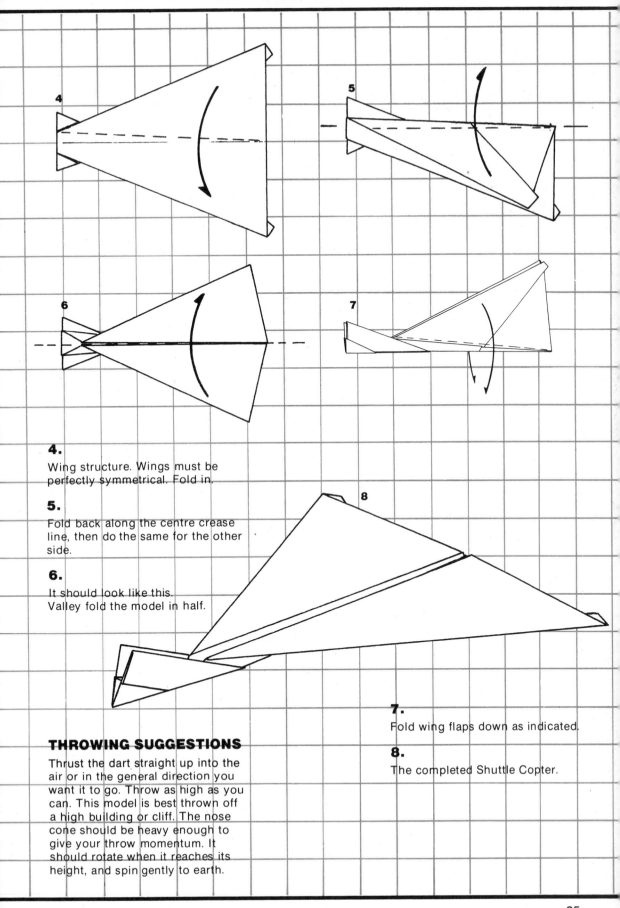

4.

Wing structure. Wings must be
perfectly symmetrical. Fold in.

5.

Fold back along the centre crease
line, then do the same for the other
side.

6.

It should look like this.
Valley fold the model in half.

7.

Fold wing flaps down as indicated.

8.

The completed Shuttle Copter.

THROWING SUGGESTIONS

Thrust the dart straight up into the
air or in the general direction you
want it to go. Throw as high as you
can. This model is best thrown off
a high building or cliff. The nose
cone should be heavy enough to
give your throw momentum. It
should rotate when it reaches its
height, and spin gently to earth.

spinner

This craft will catch anyone's eye as it streaks rudely past, spinning on its way to meet its target.

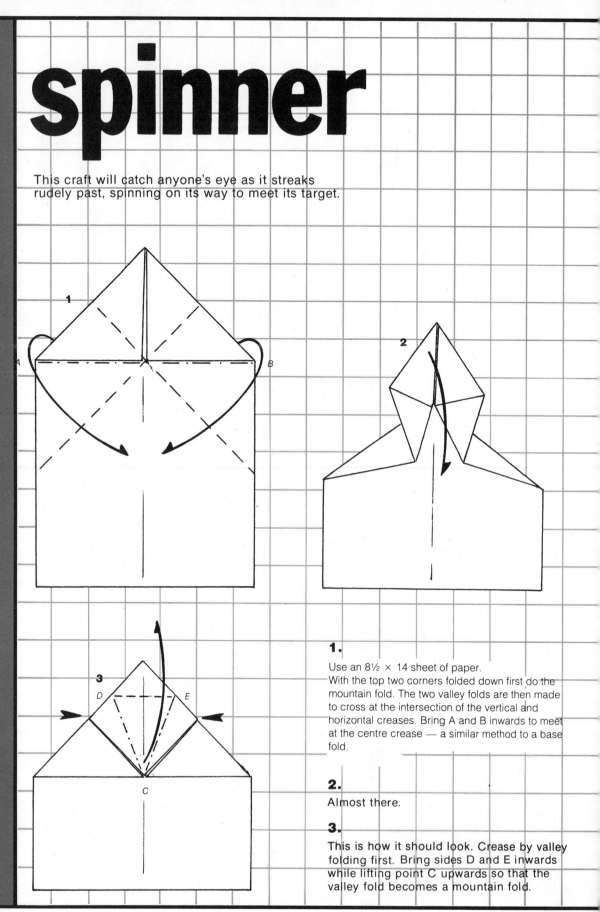

1.

Use an 8½ × 14 sheet of paper.
With the top two corners folded down first do the mountain fold. The two valley folds are then made to cross at the intersection of the vertical and horizontal creases. Bring A and B inwards to meet at the centre crease — a similar method to a base fold.

2.

Almost there.

3.

This is how it should look. Crease by valley folding first. Bring sides D and E inwards while lifting point C upwards so that the valley fold becomes a mountain fold.

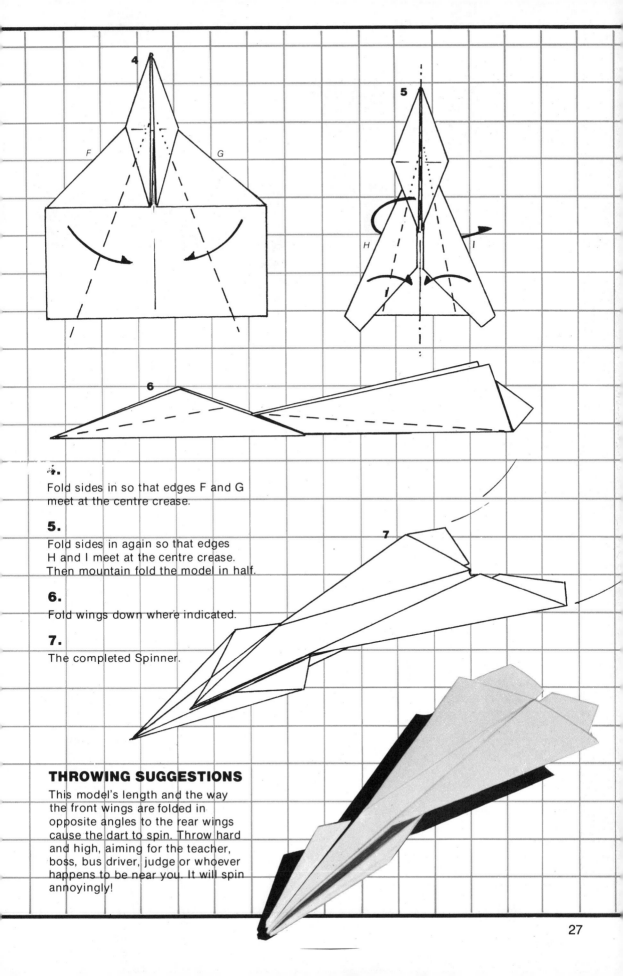

4.
Fold sides in so that edges F and G meet at the centre crease.

5.
Fold sides in again so that edges H and I meet at the centre crease. Then mountain fold the model in half.

6.
Fold wings down where indicated.

7.
The completed Spinner.

THROWING SUGGESTIONS

This model's length and the way the front wings are folded in opposite angles to the rear wings cause the dart to spin. Throw hard and high, aiming for the teacher, boss, bus driver, judge or whoever happens to be near you. It will spin annoyingly!

super stunt plane

This one will do loops, circles and fly high to catch upward breezes! Ideal for open areas — for example, the park, schoolyard, Congress and so on.

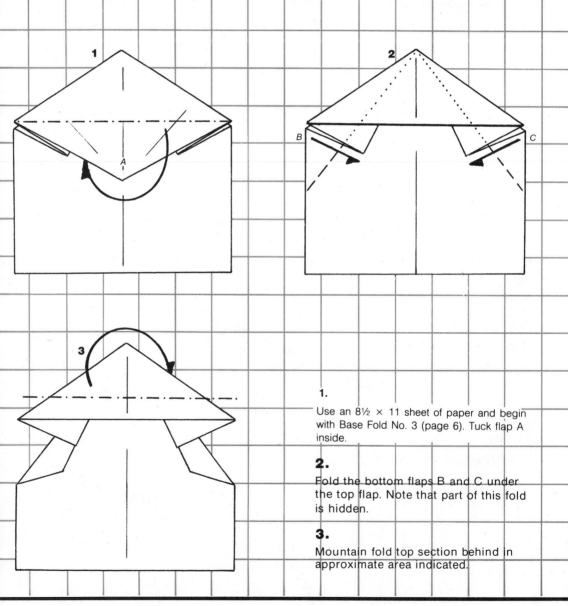

1.

Use an 8½ × 11 sheet of paper and begin with Base Fold No. 3 (page 6). Tuck flap A inside.

2.

Fold the bottom flaps B and C under the top flap. Note that part of this fold is hidden.

3.

Mountain fold top section behind in approximate area indicated.

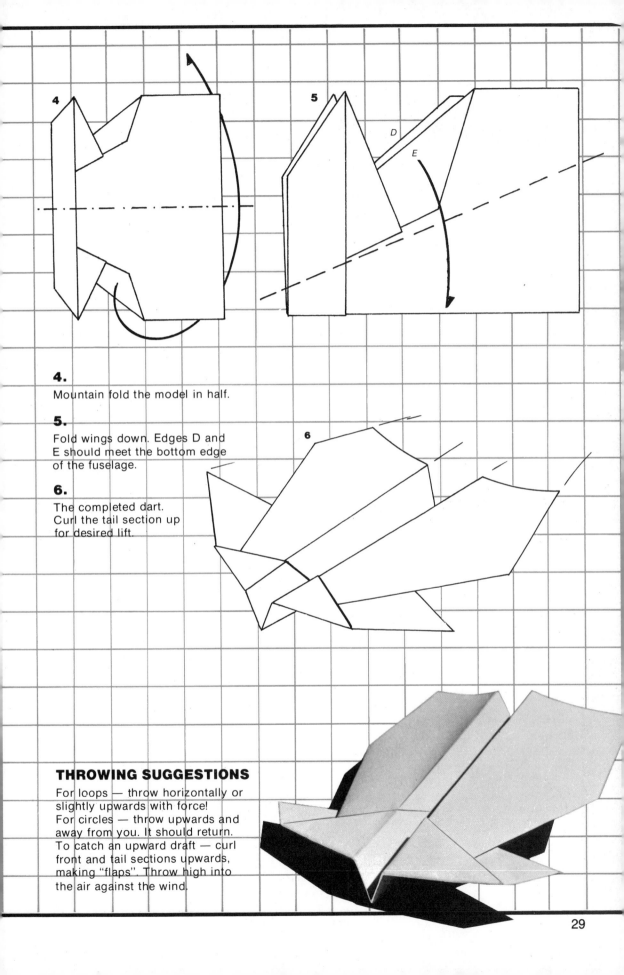

4.

Mountain fold the model in half.

5.

Fold wings down. Edges D and
E should meet the bottom edge
of the fuselage.

6.

The completed dart.
Curl the tail section up
for desired lift.

THROWING SUGGESTIONS

For loops — throw horizontally or
slightly upwards with force!
For circles — throw upwards and
away from you. It should return.
To catch an upward draft — curl
front and tail sections upwards,
making "flaps". Throw high into
the air against the wind.

jump jet

An engineering masterpiece! Imagine if every air force had a squadron of these! This model features advanced landing gear—suitable for any runway, desk, rostrum. . .

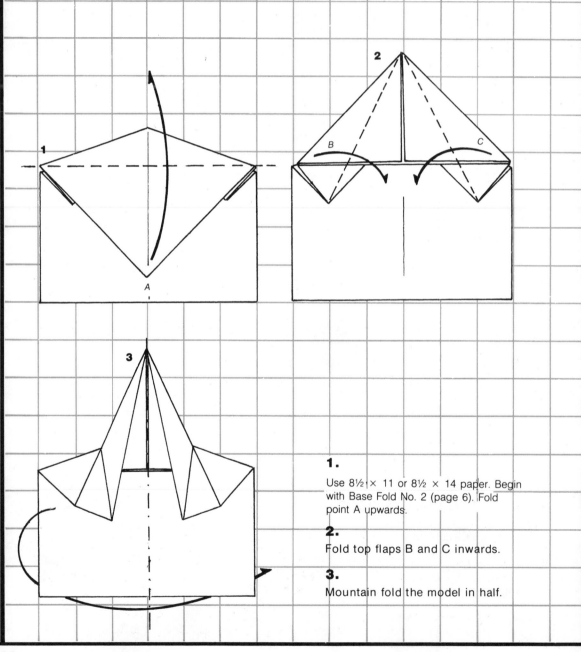

1.

Use 8½ × 11 or 8½ × 14 paper. Begin with Base Fold No. 2 (page 6). Fold point A upwards.

2.

Fold top flaps B and C inwards.

3.

Mountain fold the model in half.

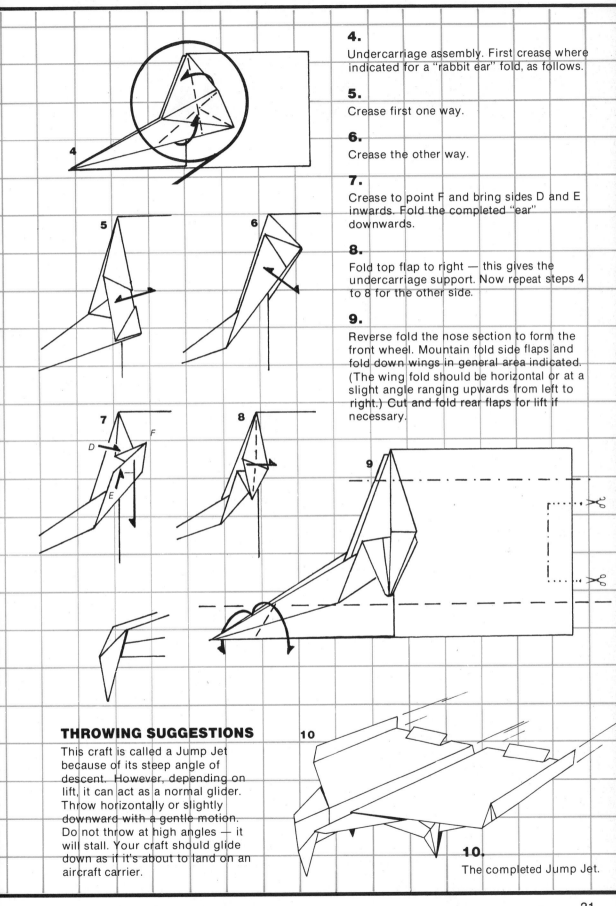

4.

Undercarriage assembly. First crease where indicated for a "rabbit ear" fold, as follows.

5.

Crease first one way.

6.

Crease the other way.

7.

Crease to point F and bring sides D and E inwards. Fold the completed "ear" downwards.

8.

Fold top flap to right — this gives the undercarriage support. Now repeat steps 4 to 8 for the other side.

9.

Reverse fold the nose section to form the front wheel. Mountain fold side flaps and fold down wings in general area indicated. (The wing fold should be horizontal or at a slight angle ranging upwards from left to right.) Cut and fold rear flaps for lift if necessary.

THROWING SUGGESTIONS

This craft is called a Jump Jet because of its steep angle of descent. However, depending on lift, it can act as a normal glider. Throw horizontally or slightly downward with a gentle motion. Do not throw at high angles — it will stall. Your craft should glide down as if it's about to land on an aircraft carrier.

10.

The completed Jump Jet.

concorde

A unique aircraft that will catch anyone's eye as it gracefully glides to a soft landing.

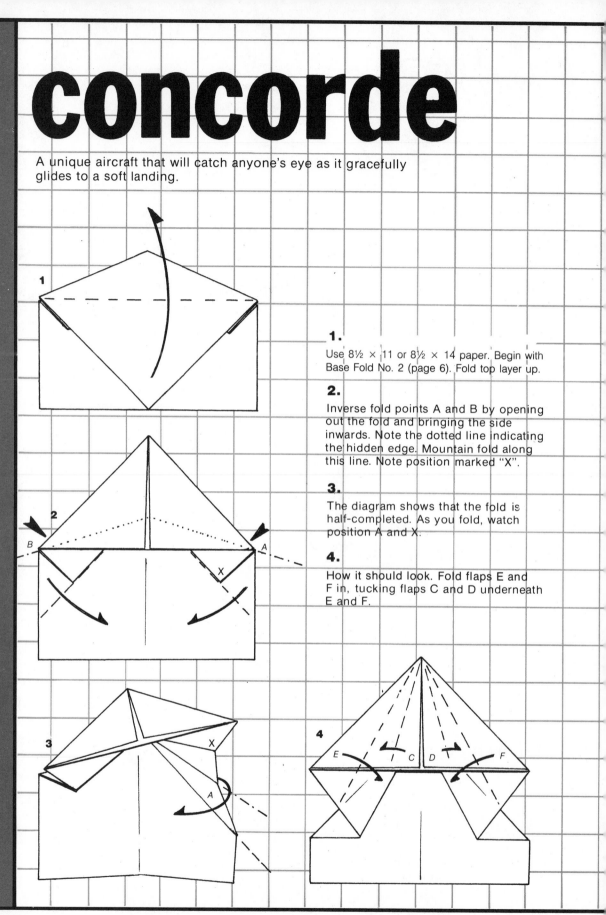

1.

Use 8½ × 11 or 8½ × 14 paper. Begin with Base Fold No. 2 (page 6). Fold top layer up.

2.

Inverse fold points A and B by opening out the fold and bringing the side inwards. Note the dotted line indicating the hidden edge. Mountain fold along this line. Note position marked "X".

3.

The diagram shows that the fold is half-completed. As you fold, watch position A and X.

4.

How it should look. Fold flaps E and F in, tucking flaps C and D underneath E and F.

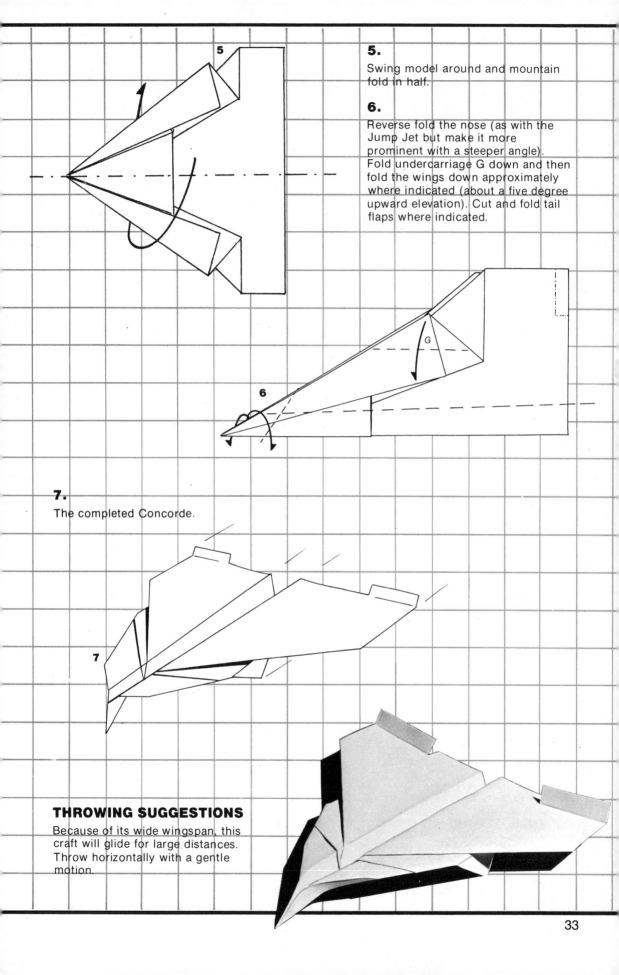

5.

Swing model around and mountain fold in half.

6.

Reverse fold the nose (as with the Jump Jet but make it more prominent with a steeper angle). Fold undercarriage G down and then fold the wings down approximately where indicated (about a five degree upward elevation). Cut and fold tail flaps where indicated.

7.

The completed Concorde.

THROWING SUGGESTIONS

Because of its wide wingspan, this craft will glide for large distances. Throw horizontally with a gentle motion.

simple stunt plane

A simple yet versatile craft that will be a nuisance to anyone in its path.

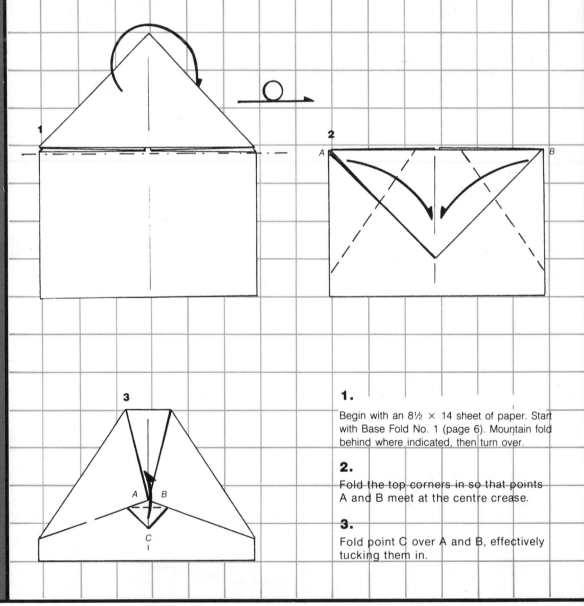

1.

Begin with an 8½ × 14 sheet of paper. Start with Base Fold No. 1 (page 6). Mountain fold behind where indicated, then turn over.

2.

Fold the top corners in so that points A and B meet at the centre crease.

3.

Fold point C over A and B, effectively tucking them in.

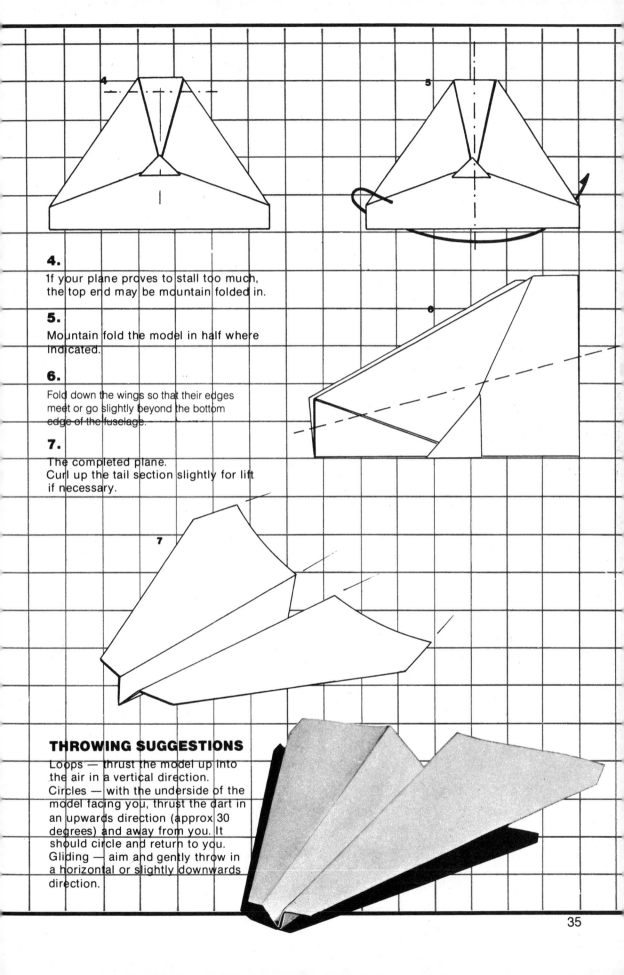

4.

If your plane proves to stall too much, the top end may be mountain folded in.

5.

Mountain fold the model in half where indicated.

6.

Fold down the wings so that their edges meet or go slightly beyond the bottom edge of the fuselage.

7.

The completed plane.
Curl up the tail section slightly for lift if necessary.

THROWING SUGGESTIONS

Loops — thrust the model up into the air in a vertical direction.
Circles — with the underside of the model facing you, thrust the dart in an upwards direction (approx 30 degrees) and away from you. It should circle and return to you.
Gliding — aim and gently throw in a horizontal or slightly downwards direction.

Advanced Aircraft

air hopper

*A graceful glider that will
"flap" its wings and hop
through the air like a butterfly.*

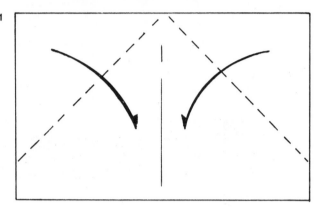

1.

*Use a sheet of 8½ × 11 or 8½ ×
14 paper. Remember that in most
cases you should fold it in half
first to make a crease. In this
case, have the paper horizontally
facing you. Fold the top corners
down.*

2.

*Fold the top point down to
meet the bottom edge.*

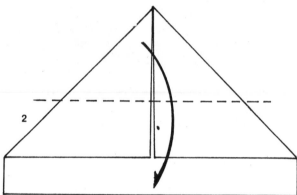

3.

*Tuck your finger under point
A, bringing point B over to the
centre crease, noting valley
and mountain folds involved.*

4.

*Halfway there. Do the same
for the other side.*

5.

*Fold the centre point up, then
mountain fold in half.*

6.

*Fold wings down in both
positions indicated. If you
want a straight (non-stalling)
glider fold down along only
one of the lines indicated to
determine stability (see
asterisk).*

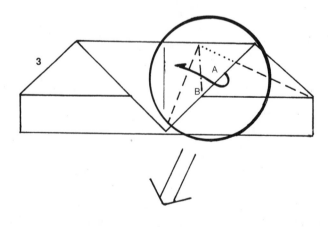

7.

The completed Air Hopper.

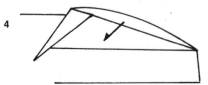

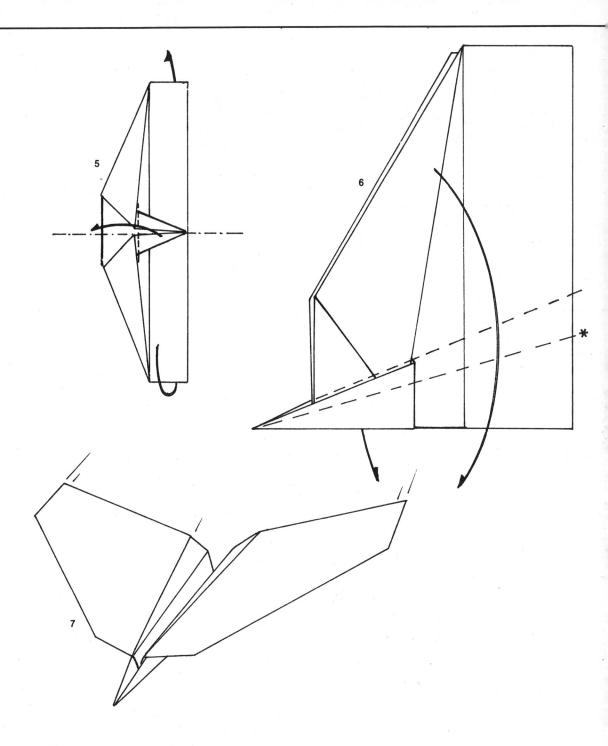

Throwing Suggestions

For loops — using heavier and more rigid paper, throw hard and high into the air.

Alternatively, you can let it glide from a high spot, say, from the back row of an opera house, and it will hop up and down, annoyingly distracting the conductor and everyone else.

stunt fly

This beast can be either a menace to fellow students, or a graceful glider, flying over to perch on your shoulder or someone's mortarboard!

1.
Use 8½ × 11 paper only (or shorten a piece of 8½ × 14). Fold in half upwards.

2.
Valley fold in the general area indicated.

3.
Place your finger under A, bringing the flap over to the right. Note the hidden section of the valley fold.

4.
Fold end several times (approximately eight or nine times depending on weight distribution factor).

5.
Fold in half.

6.
Bring wings down. Note hidden fold detail. Make a small "rabbit ear" kink in the forward section so that the centre tail can remain upright.

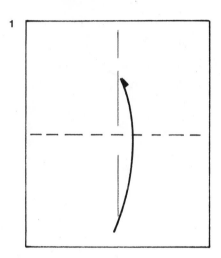

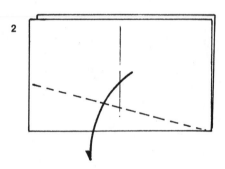

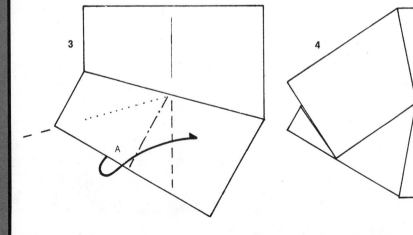

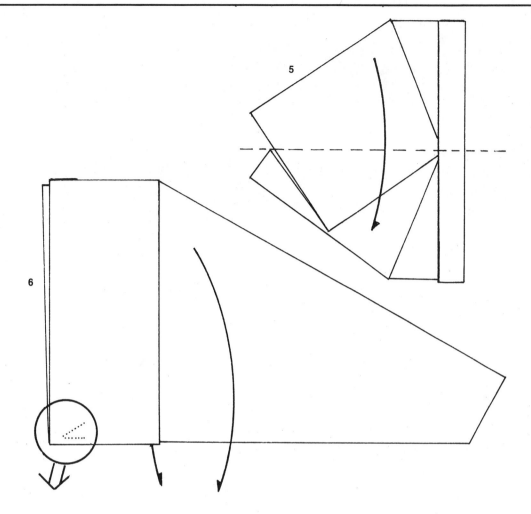

Throwing Suggestions

Make sure your model is perfectly symmetrical. To make it return to you in a vertical circle, grasp the centre-forward section with the underside facing you. Lift it up and away from you. It should loop. To make a horizontal circle, with underside facing you, throw upwards at a 30-degree angle away from you. This is quite a versatile creature that will have nature lovers intrigued by its graceful maneuverability. If it lands on your desk — don't swat it!

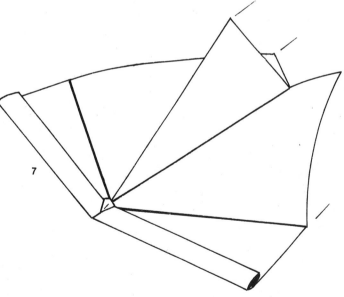

7.
The completed Stunt Fly.

elasto-kinetic jet
(sling shooter)

You're sitting calmly in the classroom.
Mathematical figures are flying through your mind as you try to solve the equation before the exam ends. Suddenly white lightning soars past you, striking the examiner right between the eyes! Lightning? No! It was that fat jerk sitting behind you with his Elasto-Kinetic Jet.

You don't need to be a math genius to make this dart!

1.
Crease and unfold the corners on your 8½ × 14 sheet of paper.

2.
Fold corners so that they meet the original crease.

3.
Fold the new edges in so that they meet the centre crease.

4.
Fold once again to meet the centre crease.

5.
Fold point to meet side edge.

6.
Fold edge twice for weight factor. Then mountain fold in half.

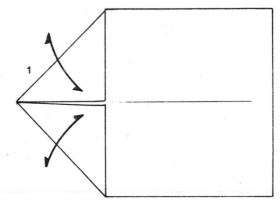

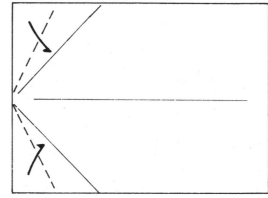

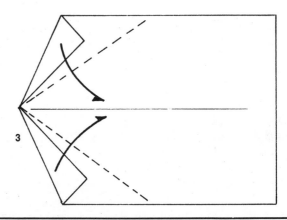

7.
Note point A. This ensures that the centre fuselage is tough enough to withstand stress upon launching. Next cut out small section where indicated and fold down wings. You may wish to add side flaps for more stability. Curl up wings for lift if necessary.

8.
The completed Elasto-Kinetic Jet.

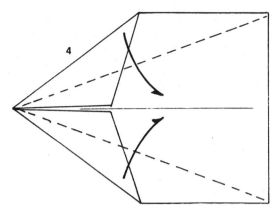

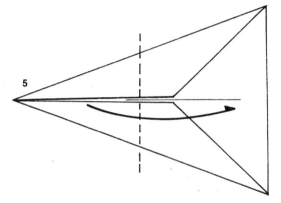

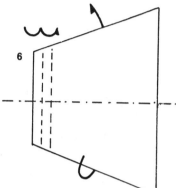

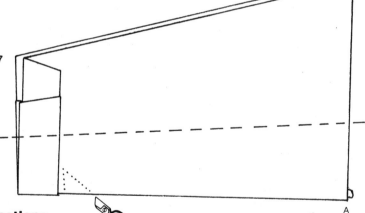

Throwing Suggestions
Hook an average-size rubber band in the cut-out section and with your fingers grasp section A (shown in diagram 7). Stretch back and let go. If you add more lift at the rear tail section and aim high, you can do an exceptionally fast loop . . . just like Buck Rogers!

(NOTE: Works best when drawn back across your arm, using the arm as a "launching strip.")
strip .)

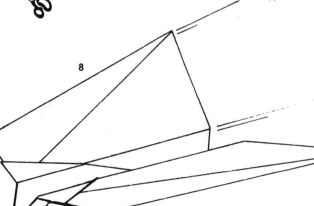

stingray glider

When I threw one of these at
work one day, it became stuck
at the top of a door. It
happened to be the door to a
management conference. As
the boss opened the door the
glider flew off and landed on
the main desk. I wonder what
the management think their
employees do all day!

1.
Fold corners on your sheet of 8½
× 11 or 8½ × 14 paper.

2.
Fold edges in to meet centre
crease.

3.
Stair-step fold where
indicated.

4.
Place finger inside point A and
bring edge across to meet
centre crease (see Air Hopper
for similar fold).

5.
Almost there. Do the same for
the other side.

6.
Now mountain fold in half.

7.
Fold wings down.

8.
The completed Stingray
Glider. Add tail lift by curling
up wings if necessary.

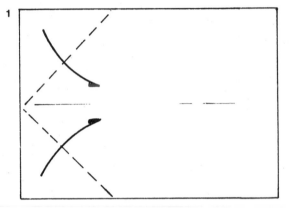

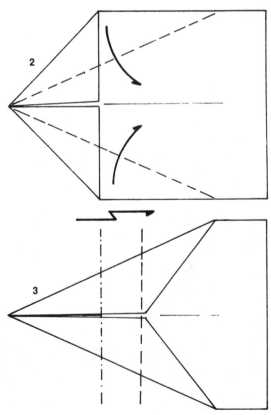

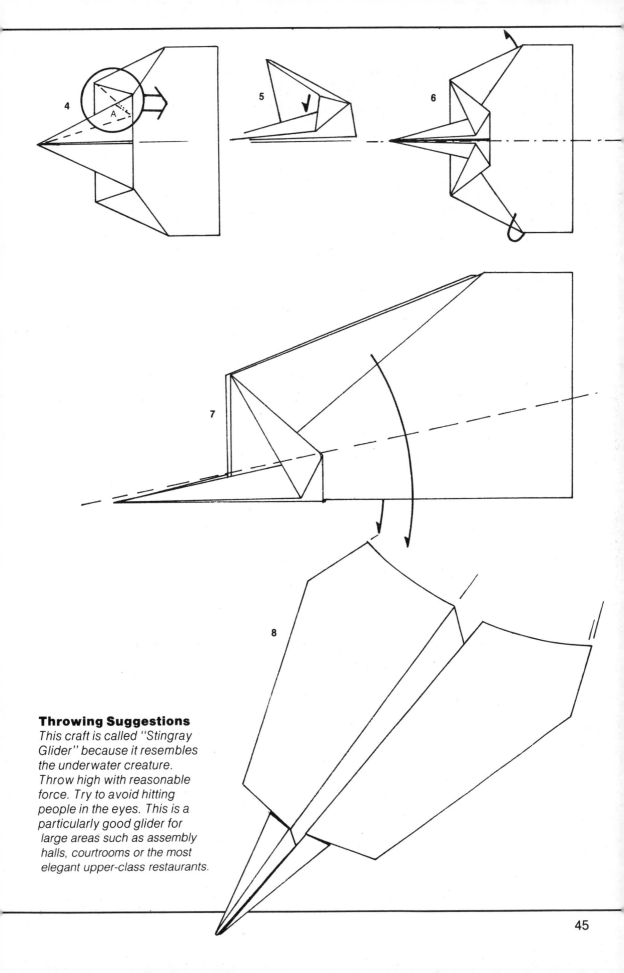

Throwing Suggestions
This craft is called "Stingray
Glider" because it resembles
the underwater creature.
Throw high with reasonable
force. Try to avoid hitting
people in the eyes. This is a
particularly good glider for
large areas such as assembly
halls, courtrooms or the most
elegant upper-class restaurants.

winged-keel glider

(controversial)

A controversial design that will win the hearts of many if ever someone comes up with an America's Cup Air Race (maybe it could compete with a Perth Plate used as a frisbee)! This is an original one-piece-of-paper design that can catch those high sea breezes and make a winner of anyone who folds it.

1.
Fold corners on your sheet of 8½ × 14 paper.

2.
Fold edges in to meet centre crease.

3.
Stair-step fold where indicated.

4.
Make a big "rabbit ear."

5.
Detailed diagram of the completed "rabbit ear."

6.
Keel section. Make a "rabbit for weight distribution factor. Then mountain fold in half.

7.
Keel section. Make a "rabbit-ear" fold, bringing point A upwards and parallel to the hull . . . er . . . fuselage of the craft. Add side flaps and tail flaps for stability and lift.

8.
The completed Winged-Keel Glider.

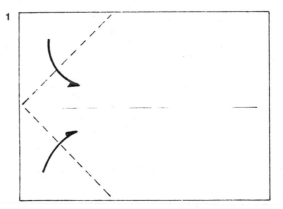

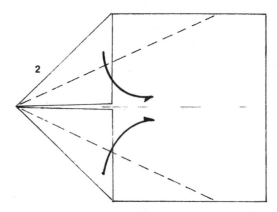

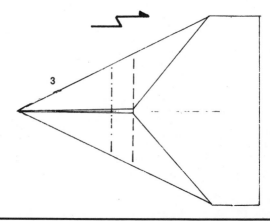

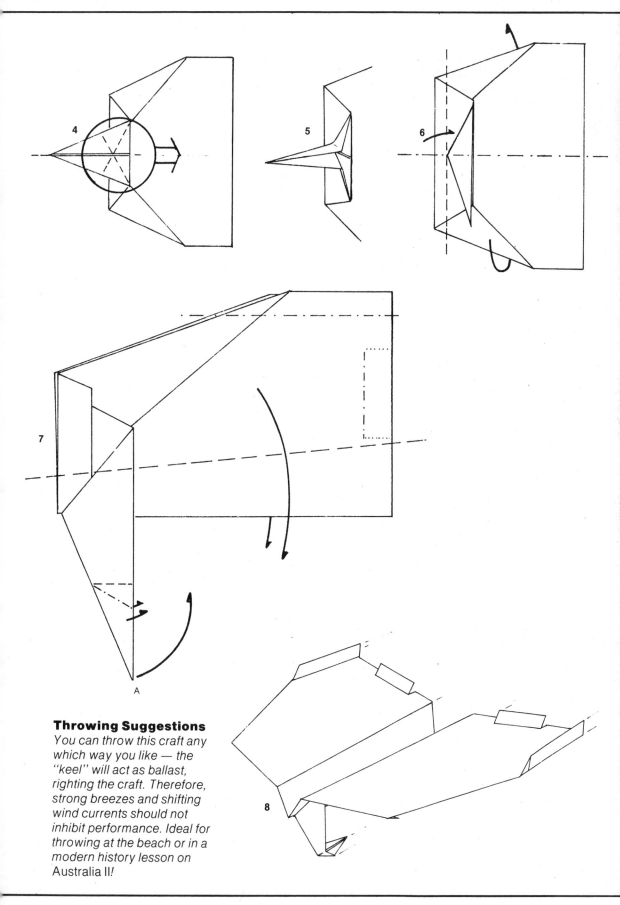

Throwing Suggestions

You can throw this craft any which way you like — the "keel" will act as ballast, righting the craft. Therefore, strong breezes and shifting wind currents should not inhibit performance. Ideal for throwing at the beach or in a modern history lesson on Australia II!

ufo

I call this model a UFO simply
because I don't know what
else to call it! Perhaps it could
be something out of Star Trek?
Often the weirdest-looking
craft can perform
outstandingly well and this
model is no exception.

1.
Use a sheet of 8½ × 11 or 8½ ×
14 paper horizontally facing you.
Make a centre crease and then
fold the top end down five to
seven times at approximately ⁵⁄₁₆
inch width each time. You may
change these specifications
depending on required weight
and lift.

2.
Fold in half.

3.
At approximately one-third of
the distance from left to right,
cut along dotted line and fold
flap across, making sure point
A meets edge (point B). Do the
same on the other side.

4.
Add side flaps and tail flaps
and fold wings down. Now for
the tricky bit: forward wings
must be locked together.

5.
Detailed view. Open up point
C and slide in section D-E
(hidden fold). It should tuck in
nicely and hold the forward
section firmly.

6.
The completed UFO.

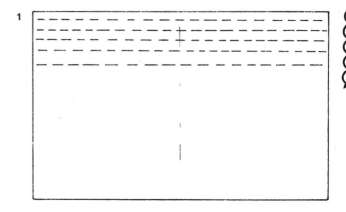

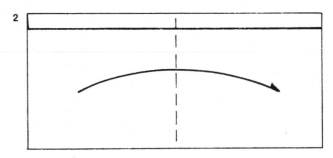

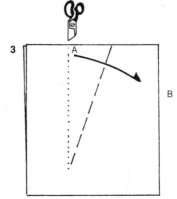

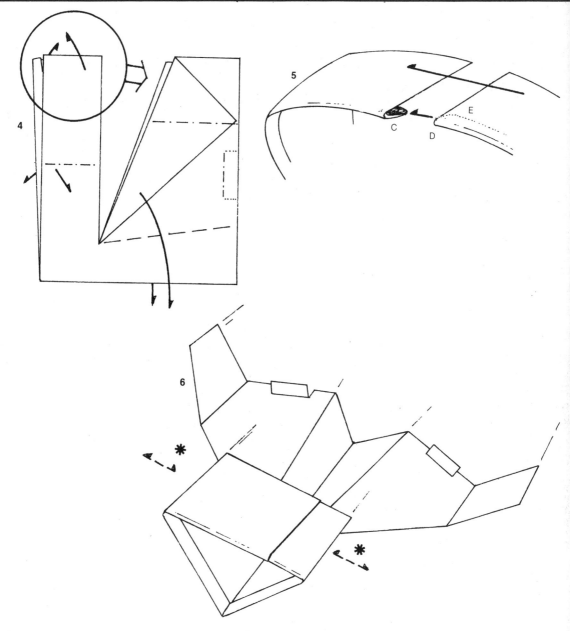

Throwing Suggestions

The wing section can be widened or shortened depending on the stability and angle of descent you require (see asterisks on diagram 6). A versatile craft indeed.

Place your forefinger inside the tail section of the fuselage, with your thumb underneath the tail section. Let your craft go on a slight downward grade. If symmetry is good, it will glide magnificently to meet a straight target . . . perhaps a teacher?

starfighter

This is the perfect craft for those who love science fiction! Imagine throwing one of these in the cinema while *Return of the Jedi* is showing. The audience will like the movie, but they'll just love the live-action scene when your Starfighter streaks down the aisle!

1.

Begin with an 8½ × 14 sheet horizontally facing you. Fold the bottom corners up and behind.

2.

Fold the top edge over six times at approximately ⅜ inch intervals.

3.

Fold A across to meet centre crease along valley fold B. Do the same for D and C. Make centre folds where indicated to form fuselage.

4.

With model turned over and the underside facing you, feed point E inside point F. Continue to push inwards for about 1⅛ inches.

5.

Larger sectional view. This is how it should look. Now make a crease fold in the centre and bring in the sides of the craft as shown in the finished plane (diagram 6).

6.

The completed Starfighter. Lengthen or shorten wingspan to determine best performance (see *UFO*).

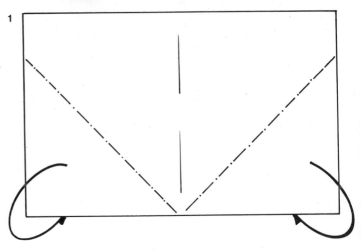

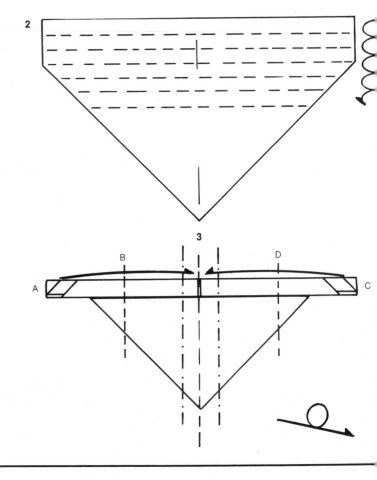

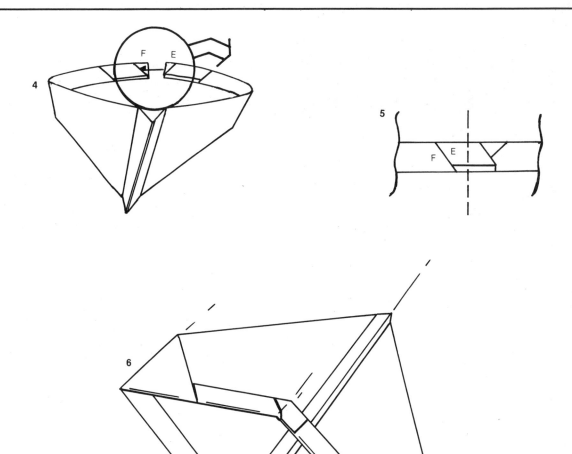

4

F E

5

F E

6

Throwing Suggestions
*Hold the fuselage with finger
and thumb and throw high with
moderate force. It may loop if
you so desire, or glide
magnificently when thrown gently.
Perhaps George Lucas could use
this design in his next Hollywood
set?*

stunt glider

A good outdoor craft that can glide-circle, do loops and handle strong breezes without being toppled. It resembles a flying arrow — something that will stand out from the usual paper glider.

1.
Crease fold where indicated, then fold the sides inwards as if you were making a base fold. A heavier 8½ × 14 sheet is preferable.

2.
Almost there.

3.
Fold top point down, tucking the two side flaps inside the top flap.

4.
Almost there.

5.
Fold in half.

6.
Fold down wings and add side flaps.

7.
The completed Stunt Glider.

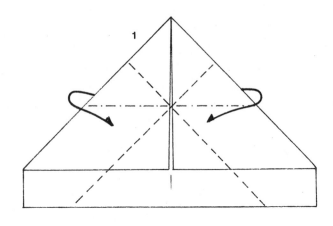

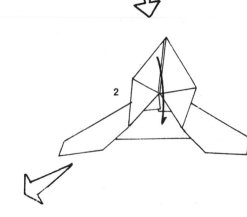

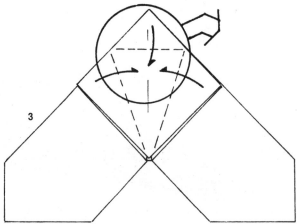

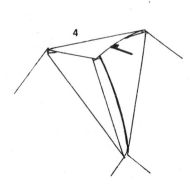

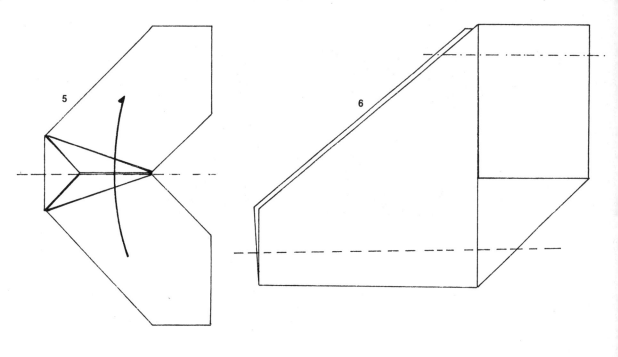

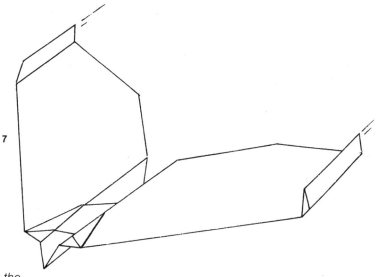

Throwing Suggestions

Throw hard and high into the air and against the wind. Depending on wind strengths it should loop or catch an upper air current and glide away. With the underside facing you, you can throw upwards at a 30-degree angle to make it circle. Don't forget — practice makes perfect!

*(**NOTE:** Birds seem to love this particular design. I threw mine high one day and a kookaburra swooped down to investigate, following its glide path.)*

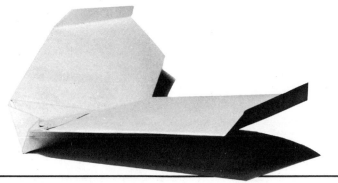

runway skimmer

An amazing glider with a folded undercarriage that ensures a somewhat interesting landing upon a teacher's desk. As it lands upon a smooth surface it skims and flies even further!

1.
Begin with a sheet of 8½ × 11 and fold Paper Plane Base Fold No. 1. Fold top flap up where indicated, noting centre fold.

2.
Almost complete.

3.
Fold top end behind.

4.
Mountain fold in half.

5.
Fold down wings, undercarriage and feet. Add lift to tail section if necessary. For more direction, add side flaps.

6.
The completed Runway Skimmer.

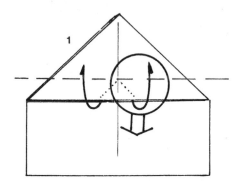

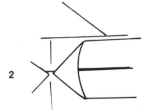

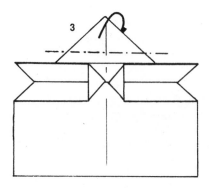

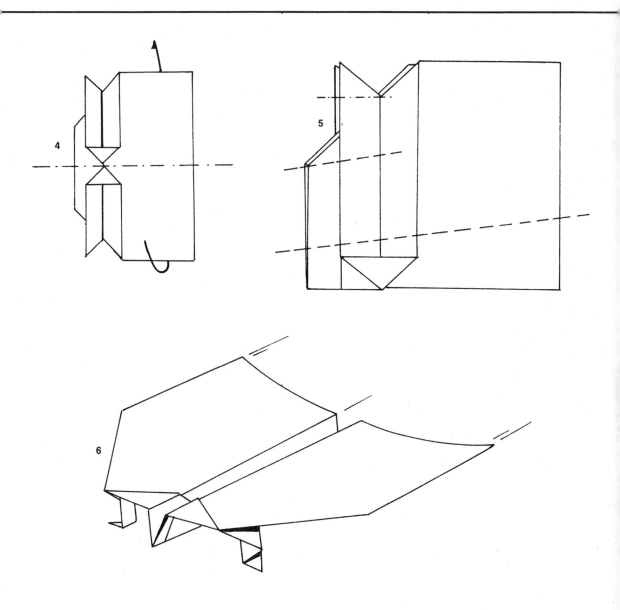

Throwing Suggestions

Let go gently in a downward motion. If it lands on a smooth surface, say, a teacher's desk or the manager's desk (which would be much longer) the spring action on the undercarriage will "bounce" the craft up; and probably over the edge.

dart attack

The war is on! Paper darts are flying everywhere, throughout the lecture hall, as the students demonstrate what they think of the lecturer! Now imagine you had the ultimate in paper fighting "machines" — something with gun turrets or landing gear that would annoyingly stick in someone's hair. The fighter of your imagination is only as far away as the piece of paper in front of you!

1.
Begin with Paper Plane Base Fold No. 1. Make a "rabbit ear" on the top right-hand flap.

2.
Almost there. Do the same for the other side.

3.
Open out the "rabbit ear" by tucking your finger inside and folding where indicated.

4.
Fold top half down, then fold across to the right. Do the same for the other side.

5.
Fold the two sides inwards.

6.
Mountain fold in half.

7.
Reverse fold the "feet" or guns where indicated and open outwards. Cut where indicated on tail fuselage, then inverse fold to make a fin. Fold down wings and side flaps where indicated.

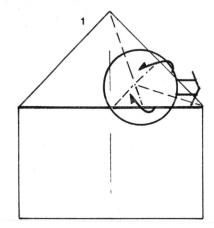

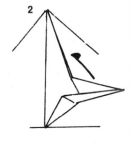

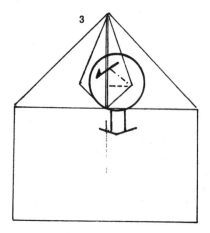

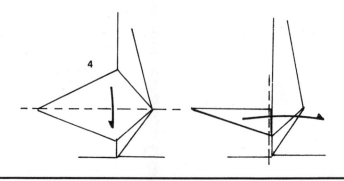

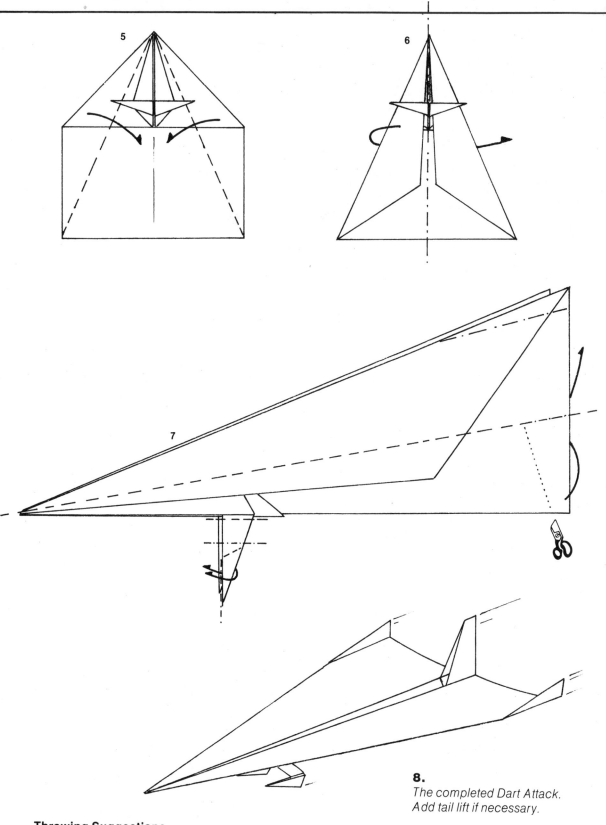

8.
The completed Dart Attack.
Add tail lift if necessary.

Throwing Suggestions
Throw hard and high, aiming
for anything that dares to take
you on!

dive bomber

Just like Buck Rogers! This craft will make a huge swooping dive, picking up momentum and gathering lift. The model forward guns add a more realistic effect.

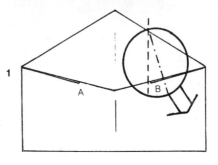

1.

Begin with Paper Plane Base Fold No. 3: 8½ × 11 or 8½ × 14 paper is ideal. Note your base fold points A and B. Run a vertical valley fold up from these points and then make a fold similar to a "rabbit ear" by tucking your finger inside the top flap and folding where indicated.

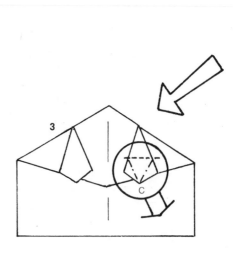

2.

Almost there.

3.

Once this fold is done on both sides, you can lift the flap (point C) upwards and fold where indicated.

4.

Almost there.

5.

Turn model over.

6.

Valley fold where indicated.

7.

Valley fold top section down where indicated. The two points behind should flip up.

8.

Now mountain fold in half.

9.

Mountain and valley fold wings where indicated.

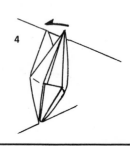

10.

The completed Dive Bomber.

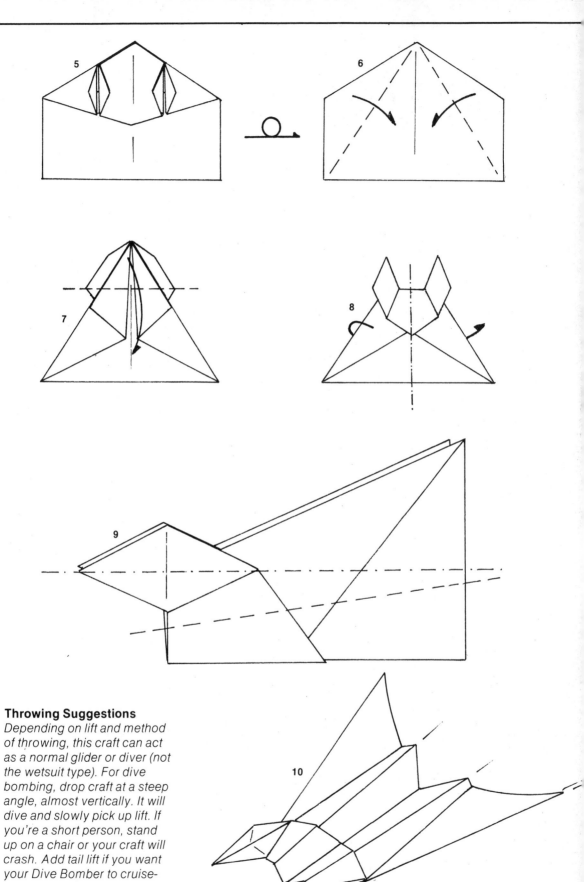

Throwing Suggestions

Depending on lift and method of throwing, this craft can act as a normal glider or diver (not the wetsuit type). For dive bombing, drop craft at a steep angle, almost vertically. It will dive and slowly pick up lift. If you're a short person, stand up on a chair or your craft will crash. Add tail lift if you want your Dive Bomber to cruise-glide instead.

heliglider

You'd freak if you saw this hovering in the school assembly area! That's because this craft is a technological masterpiece representing a combination of helicopter and glider; yet it is surprisingly simple. Folded correctly, it will prove a unique talking piece for physics students and others.

1.
Begin with an 8½ × 14 sheet of paper. Cut an approximately ¾ inch strip off the tail end, but don't throw it out! Fold top corners in.

2.
Fold sides in.

3.
Fold top point down to meet bottom edge.

4.
Folding where indicated, edge A must meet the centre crease. When this is established points C and B will fold across.

5.
Like so — almost there.

6.
Fold top end down two or three times depending on the weight you wish to achieve. Then fold in half.

7.
Note hidden folds. Inverse fold the centre point upwards. This is the centre "propeller" shaft. On final folding, you must work out balance. It is critical in the performance of your craft. Therefore, the centre shaft can be folded from a more forward of aft position.

8.
What it should look like. Fold the wing across and leave aside for the moment.

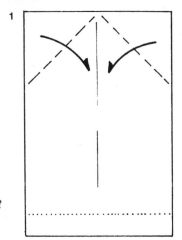

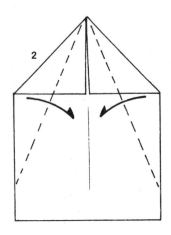

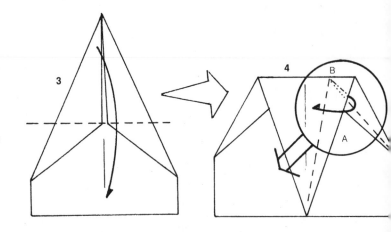

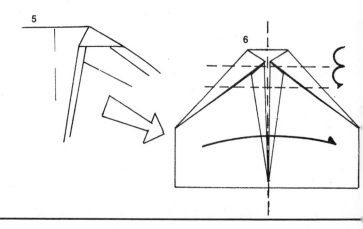

9.

Now, remember the paper strip? If it hasn't wound up in the backyard barbecue, grab it and fold in half as shown in diagram 9. Fold where indicated at opposite angles leaving some vertical headroom at the top.

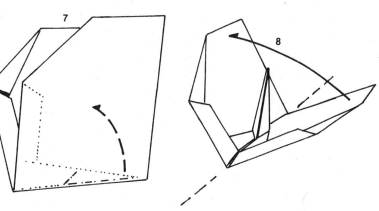

10.

It should look something like this.

11.

Fold down wings on your glider section where indicated.

12.

Now grab a pin from the nearest tax form or sewing box. Make sure it's an average everyday type about ¾ inch long with a head on it. Feed the pin through the centre of your rotor blade (note the two dots) two or three times to secure it together. Then feed it through the top of the shaft two or three times making sure the rotor can rotate smoothly. Add side flaps to the craft for more stability if you wish. Slight tail lift if necessary.

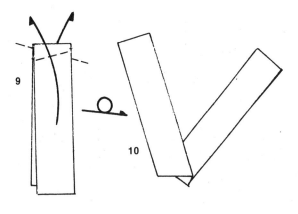

13.

The completed Heliglider.

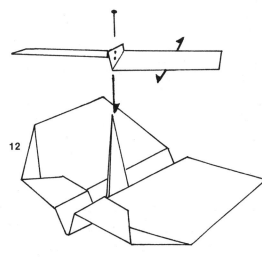

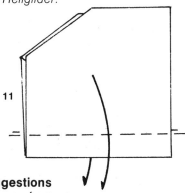

Throwing Suggestions

Throw gently away from you in a slight downward motion with the rotor blades facing horizontally towards you. For better performance, give the rotor blades a slight curl upwards as shown in diagram 12. This will reinforce the blade, preventing it being "floppy." Also note that the centre of the rotor blade must be kept secured by the pin.

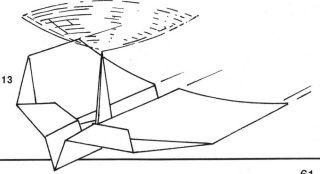

space shuttle

Now here is an inexpensive way to build and fly your space shuttle without spending a fortune on silicone matting or having to replace the occasional missing tile!

1.

Make a sight crease fold in the centre of a sheet of 8½ × 14 paper. Now fold the bottom side in to make another crease fold. Tear or cut off the strip of paper, making the foolscap sheet proportionately longer.

2.

Make a new centre crease and fold Paper Plane Base Fold No. 1 as shown. Fold the left hand corners then fold right hand sides in as shown — under the top flap.

3.

Stair-step fold where indicated and make a "rabbit-ear" on the other end of the craft.

4.

How it should look. Detailed fold shown.

5.

Fold flap, flattening point A.

6.

The asterisk indicates how the undercarriage is folded upon completion of your craft. You may wish to use your own ingenuity to make the undercarriage more complicated.

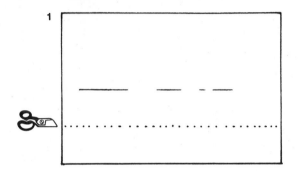

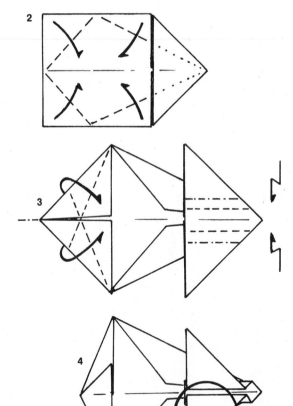

7.

Fold end two or three times depending on correct weight needed for flight. Then fold the left side "rabbit-ear" behind. After you have done this, valley fold in half.

8.

Fold wings up at a slight angle and then fold the undercarriage as shown in diagram 6.

9.

The completed Space Shuttle. Tail lift should not be necessary, though extra weight may be needed if your craft stalls. Try inversing the forward nose section at an angle or adjust undercarriage to reduce drag.

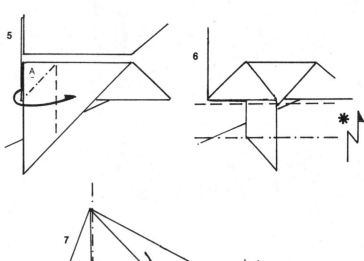

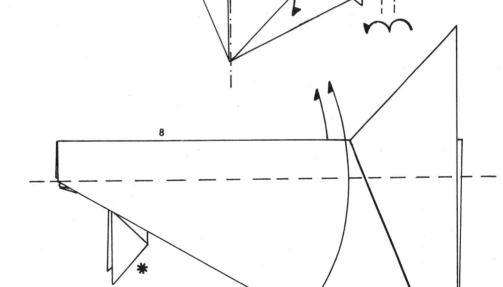

Throwing Suggestions

Have your craft at a slight downward angle, holding the tail fin with your finger and thumb. With slight motion, let it drop — it will glide to a smooth touchdown.

Ideal for lecture halls if the discussion is on space technology!

kamikaze water bomber

Wow! A flying projectile (you can use it only once, hence "Kamikaze") that will have umpires storming off the baseball field or politicians crossing the floor.

1.
Begin with an 8½ × 14 sheet but take approximately 1⅛ inches off the side of the sheet to make it proportionately longer. See diagram 1 p. 62.

2.
Fold Paper Plane Base Fold No. 1. Fold the flaps in.

3.
Fold flaps where indicated.

4.
Tuck point A inside the pocket B as shown in direction of arrow.

5.
Like so.

6.
Once you've made this fold to the other side, fold the whole flap behind.

7.
With the model turned over, inverse fold corners.

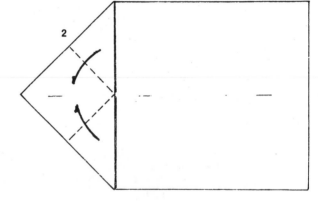

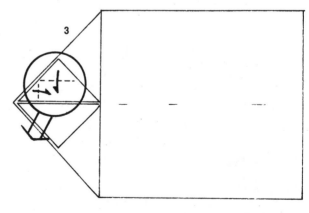

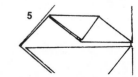